T0344511

risk |risk|

noun (pl. risks)

a situation involving exposure to danger: *all outdoor activities carry an element of risk.*

• the possibility that something unpleasant or unwelcome will happen: *reduce the risk of heart disease.*

• a person or thing regarded as likely to turn out well or badly, as specified, in a particular context or respect: *Western banks regarded Romania as a good risk.*

• a person or thing regarded as a threat or likely source of danger: *she's a security risk.*

• the possibility of financial loss: *project finance is essentially an exercise in risk management.*

Oxford English Dictionary, 3rd Ed.

IN THIS ISSUE

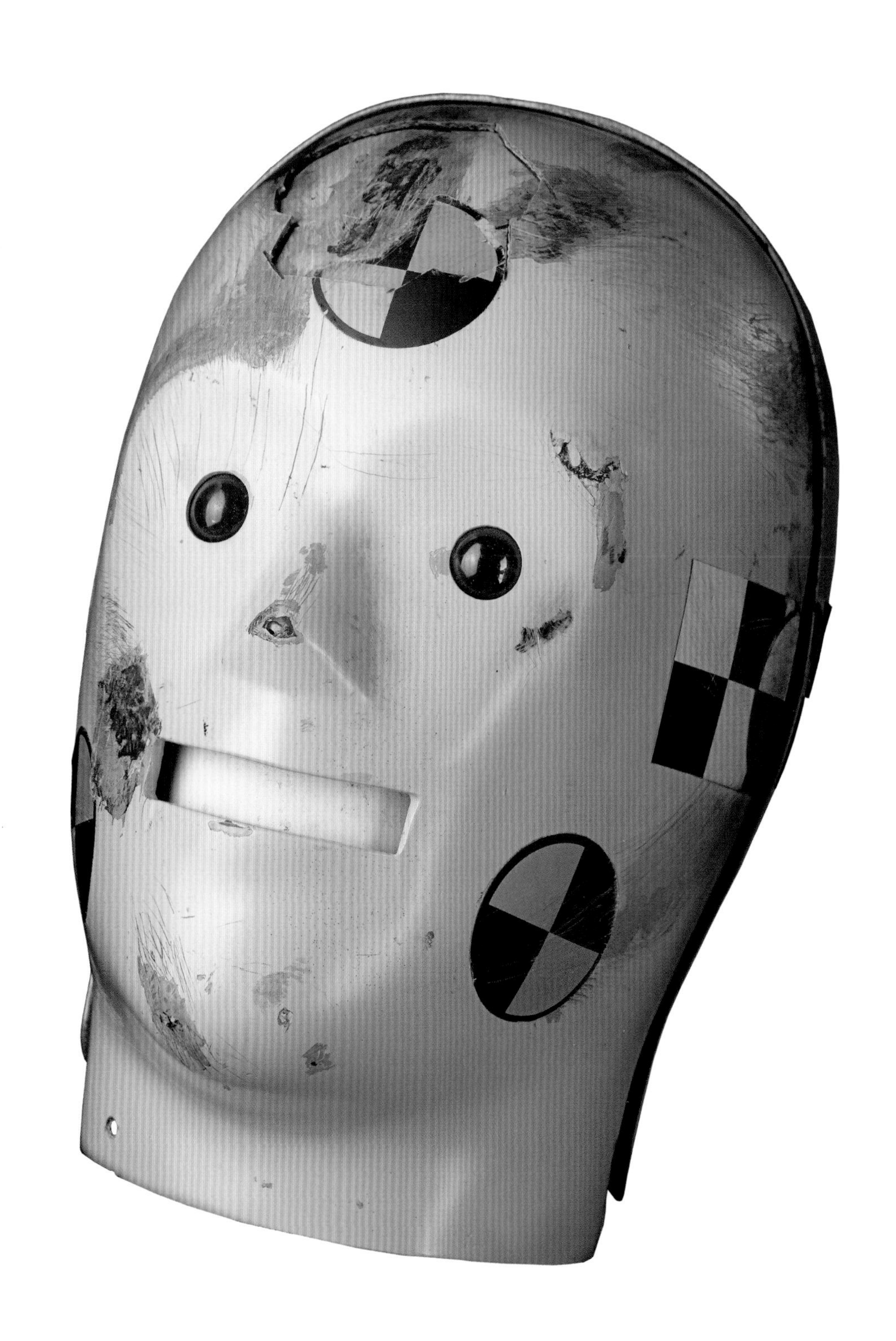

LA+ RISK EDITORIAL

The notion that modernity is inherently characterized by risk became prominent after German sociologist Ulrich Beck's publication of *Risk Society* in 1986 (English trans. 1992). Beck's seemingly simple observation was that the risks that individuals and society face, are less those of providence, and more the dystopian consequences of our own utopian strivings. In short, we are a risk to ourselves and this is both modernity's curse, and its engine of innovation. Climate change and the recognition of the Anthropocene as the entanglement of cultural and natural history, is the apotheosis of this condition.

At the turn of the millennium, there was optimism that the horrors of the 20th century's hot and cold wars were now behind us and that an emerging ecological understanding of systems could deliver us into a stable and sustainable world. That faith in reason was snuffed out with 9/11 and to this day neoliberalism and fundamentalism remain at war, with nothing much in between. Not only that, we can now see that the very notion of equilibrium implied by sustainability is incommensurate with nature as we currently understand it. That is, nature as inherently chaotic. But chaos is not the absence of order, it is an order that partially incorporates indeterminacy and uncertainty: a more nuanced form of order. Life is something tensioned between degrees of resistance to flux on the one hand, and completely "going with the flow" on the other. The risk of life teeters between the two.

In this sense, to be sustainable is not to reach stasis, but to be able to adapt to constant change, the catch-all expression for which is now 'resiliency,' and it is little wonder that in an age of extreme and rapid climate change it has emerged as a dominant design paradigm. As Matthijs Bouw alludes to in this issue, design thinking has a critical role to play in tuning cultural systems to better cope with the inherent risks of modernity's volatile political, economic, and environmental conditions. This, in short, was Andrew Zolli's thesis in 2012 when, with Anne Marie Healy, he published *Resilience: Why Things Bounce Back* and it will be of interest to LA+ readers to now see Zolli working with real-time satellite imagery as a mechanism for adaptation on a planetary scale. Also at this scale, Richard Weller overviews the risks associated with geo-engineering solutions to climate change and compares these to the risk of doing nothing.

Of course, the ice is melting and the seas are rising and much is being done on a local scale to address this. Essays by Kristina Hill, Billy Fleming, and Catherine Seavitt and Guy Nordenson examine adaptive strategies currently underway in three very different North American coastal environments. In an effort to provide a global survey of current theory and practice we invited urban geographers Jon Coaffee and Jonathan Clarke to survey resilient urban design in Europe, while geologist and planner Robert Olshansky reminds us of the importance of social resilience – the ability of some communities to adapt to natural hazards regardless of the quantitatively measured objective risk. Counterbalancing reports from the developed world, architects Stephan Kieran and James Timberlake discuss their work in Dhaka, Bangladesh – the most-densely populated city in the world and one at high risk for devastating floods and earthquakes.

Three papers approach the science of risk in different, interdisciplinary ways. The first by energy researchers Mark Alan Hughes, Cornelia Colijn, and Oscar Serpell draws an instructive comparison between the management of watersheds and energy systems in the United States to reduce service-based risk. In the second, environmental planner Allison Lassiter explores new technologies in landscape infrastructures that measure and respond to environmental risks, and in the third, epidemiologist David Waltner-Toews and landscape architect Matthew Waltner-Toews discuss an ecosystem approach to public health risks.

Taking a more contemplative approach, LA+ regular contributor philosopher Mark Kingwell opens up a political and ethical discourse of risk, while New Zealand-based landscape architect Jacky Bowring reflects on the sublime in relation to her country's "extreme landscapes" of risk. And in two very different short 'provocations' in this issue, Bernard Spiegal invites playground designers to toss out their rule-books and reconceive the city as the playground, while Thomas Oles and Phoebe Lickwar challenge design educators and students to stop managing risks and start taking them. Finally, as always, LA+ invited visual essays on the issue's theme, the most compelling of which are included at the end of this issue.

Tatum L. Hands, Richard Weller + Billy Fleming
Issue Editors

MARK KINGWELL

THE POLITICS OF RISK

Mark Kingwell is Professor of Philosophy at the University of Toronto and a contributing editor of *Harper's Magazine* in New York. His articles on politics, architecture, and art have appeared in academic journals, and mainstream publications such as *The New York Times*, *The Wall Street Journal*, and *The Guardian*. His most recent books are the linked essay collections *Unruly Voices* (2012) and *Measure Yourself Against the Earth* (2015), and a monograph about sports and culture, *Fail Better* (2017). He is currently working on a book about the politics of boredom.

+ PHILOSOPHY, POLITICAL SCIENCE

What are the political dimensions of risk? I argue that there are three distinct orders of political risk, and that they are nested in ways that have been neglected by traditional political theory and public policy alike. Only by disentangling and then seeing the complex nesting of these risk-orders will we be able to appreciate the role that risk plays in geopolitical life.

The most obvious order of risk is surely the consequences generated by at-risk populations around the globe. For obvious historical and political reasons, large chunks of the Earth's population daily face risks unknown to the rest of the world. Food security, for example—the ability to count on regular and affordable supplies of daily sustenance—is a concern so far from the minds of even the poorest North Americans and Europeans that it can be difficult to imagine life in sub-Saharan Africa or parts of Asia.

Potable water is an even more vivid example, since even the most privileged among the planet's seven billion human inhabitants now realize that a continued supply of fresh and non-toxic water is imperiled. The tainted-water scandals in Flint, Michigan and Walkerton, Ontario are timely, if also nasty, reminders of how fragile the global fresh-water table is even in the developed world. Elsewhere, the scandal is a daily reality. Physical risks of this sort pose associated dangers over supply and control. Violence is more prevalent in nations where resource scarcity is an ongoing problem.[1]

And so those persons who find themselves living under such conditions have traditionally felt that they have legitimate demands on those with the resources to alleviate actual and possible harms. This is the moral basis of claims for disaster relief, poverty and disease control, food security, and reduction of yawning wealth inequality. Let's call this cluster of issues 'Order-One Risk.'

But there is already a hint of another dimension of risk in play here. The inhabitants of risky populations and areas did not choose their positions; it is the result of a particularly nasty feature of what is known as the 'birthright lottery.' Where and who I am born to be is a matter of luck, but it is luck of an especially far-reaching kind. Thus, farther upstream of these urgent questions of relief and aid is another dimension of risk, concerning the distribution of risk itself. What are the politics here?

Most risks can be divided into those chosen and unchosen. In contrast to other situations where choice is a factor in human affairs, when it comes to the basic situation of life—where and who I am—we tend to discount chosen risk and inflate unchosen risk. That is, we tend to minimize aid or even punish those who suffer from the outcomes of risky choices, and help or at least consider helping those shouldering the burdens of unchosen risk. So, for example, we typically have little sympathy for a gambler or property speculator who went all-in on some chancy bet, and ended up losing. "Tough luck," we say, implying that the bad luck was, in effect, purchased

0 32 15 19 4 21 2 25 17 34 6 27 13 36 11 30 8 23 10 5 24 16 33 1 20 14 31 9 22 18 29 7 28 12 35 3 26

by the speculator or gambler as a matter of conscious agency. But when risk is distributed both unevenly and without consent, we think it right to favor the unfavored. When someone, through no fault of their own, is born to misfortune in a degraded environment with imminent prospects of struggle and violence, we do not usually–unless we are ruthless to the point of cynicism–call that tough luck. We call it, instead, misfortune, and consider it to have some moral traction on us. The gambler has no one to blame but himself, we think, unless we subscribe to social-influence or addiction theories of a far-reaching kind.

But even the addiction narrative usually involves elements of choice and responsibility – we do not, as when Homer Simpson observes the breakdown of wife Marge in a Vegas gambling spree, blame an interior monster called "Gamblor," who has taken possession of her soul. If addiction is a monster, it is a metaphorical one, and thus a beast we believe can be slain through a combination of guidance, contextual support, and willpower. Hence the most sympathetic observer of someone taking bad risks by choice will likely insist that there is always a measure of personal responsibility in play, even in those cases where robust personal autonomy has been partially compromised. Gamblers are not automatons, and choice matters even when it is complicated.[2]

By contrast, when there is no matter of choice in play–where, in fact, there cannot be–even the most grim observer will have a hard time maintaining that the risk incurred is a matter of personal responsibility. Central to this issue is not just the fact but the *supreme power* of birthright lottery. The overarching fact of human existence is that we do not choose who and where we are born, nor do we choose most of the consequences of those facts. This lottery–captured by the notion of "tell me who your parents are and I will tell you who you are"–governs the bulk of life chances for all humans. Let's call this 'Order-Two Risk,' since it generates many (or most) of the conditions considered in Order-One Risk.

Order-Two Risk can be spectral. What I mean is that smokescreens of various kinds work to conceal its political essence. For example, if you had the 'good sense' to be born to wealthy parents in the developed world, your chances of comfort, long life, and happiness are maximized. You might even begin to think that this highly contingent outcome is something you engineered out of personal virtue. Thus the spectacle of Excessive Entitlement Disorder (sometimes also called 'affluenza') whereby a lucky sod is born on third base and grows up thinking he hit a triple. Good luck is here comprehensively confused with virtue.

That baseball-derived metaphor was often used to describe former US president George W. Bush. This mediocre scion of a powerful family attended Yale University as a 'legacy' applicant – itself a traditional practice of preference that functions as a sort of frequent-flier program for the wealthy who convert their cash, in the form of reliable donations, into cachet, in the form of an Ivy League degree (I won't say education). But more than this, Bush entered the White House as president of the United States, despite being drastically underqualified, because of a network of influence that, in another context, would have landed him a comfortable chair on the New York Stock Exchange. Indeed, from the point of view of the Bush family circle, the two offices are more or less the same thing.

Such influence-peddling is offensive all by itself, but is made exponentially worse by the delusion that the resulting success was somehow earned rather than granted. There is no virtue in being born to rich parents, any more than there is vice in being born to poor ones. But these obvious facts can be hard to see through the mists of delusion that settle around wealth and power. This is the essence of Randian entitlement, that bizarre stew of anti-collectivism and aggressive individualism that suffuses the tortuous novels of Ayn Rand. Here, in *The Fountainhead* (1943) or *Atlas Shrugged* (1957), all success is purely the result of individual creativity and effort, parasitically drained by the forces of altruism, taxation, and the general good. Never mind that, in fact, there is no such success without markets, and workers, and the infrastructure that makes economies possible – not least the baseline existence of money, that collective fantasy-token of trust and cooperation.

More recently, the same phenomenon of transmuting inherited wealth into personal virtue could be observed in Donald Trump. The Republican presidential candidate liked to portray himself as a self-made man, even a man of the people, conveniently obliterating the fact that this worldly success was made possible by a hefty inheritance. The *New Yorker* satirist Andy Borowitz nailed the point with an imagined news article headlined "Trump Economic Plan Calls for Every American to Inherit Millions from Father." According to the article, Trump made a rallying speech about the economy: "'There are people at my rallies, desperate people, desperate because they want jobs,' he told his luncheon audience at the Detroit Economic Club. 'Once they inherit millions from their father, they will never want a job again.'"[3]

Such extreme cases are targets of easy satire. But political theorists have struggled with birthright lottery, in large measure because its contingencies seem so intractable. How could one ever hope to stem the tide of consequences brought about by the brute facts of birth and situation? Every post-facto justice measure would be climbing uphill against the steep grade of chance. And are we perhaps overstepping the bounds of legitimate intervention if we try to advance such measures? Perhaps there are simply some things that remain misfortunes rather than injustices?

But every conceivable distinction between misfortune and injustice is open to criticism. Is the New Orleans flood, say, merely an act of god (misfortune) or a matter of heinously bad infrastructure (injustice)? When does inept government count more than the simple bad luck of living in a drowned parish?

To answer these thorny questions, many people follow the lead of John Rawls's foundational work on justice, and have adopted versions of an 'original position.' This is an imagined choice scenario in which the specific circumstances of birth are excluded by a 'veil of ignorance,' thus freeing choosers to settle on schemes of justification and basic social structure that are fair to all.[4] Note that, when we imagine what rules of the social game we might choose if we didn't know who our parents are, the basic lottery is assumed. The uneven natural distribution of favors is what makes justice an issue in the first place.

Some critics have balked at the idea of such ignorance-based choice as the basis of legitimate social policy, but consider for a moment the core insight. If I don't know who, in particular, I am, then I really do have a basic rational stake in upholding practices of fairness in distributing goods and life chances. A simple analogy captures the point. Suppose I am asked by my mother to cut the remaining portion of a pie into two sections, one for me and one for my brother. The catch is that, while I *cut* first, he gets to *choose* first. The only rational action on my part is to opt for equal shares of the remaining pie. Any other course is self-defeating, given an assumption of basic rationality on the part of my brother (i.e., he will choose the larger piece, given the chance). The original position in effect models a complex version of this scenario: we all can do the cutting, but nobody knows who's going to get to do the choosing.

But here I want to postulate yet another order of risk. It brings together the luck of the lottery with the original-choice model's notion of consenting participants, but with a new twist. This 'Order-Three Risk' concerns the relative levels of *aversion* and *tolerance* regarding risk itself, qualities which might themselves be distributed unevenly within a population. Indeed, all evidence shows that the distribution of tolerance to risk is wildly uneven. Some people are simply more inclined to take chances–to shoulder risk–than others. Moreover, they consider this risky behavior rational.

1 See, for example, the work of Thomas Homer-Dixon, beginning with a landmark article called "Environmental Scarcities and Violent Conflict: Evidence from Cases," *International Security* 19, no. 1 (1994): 5–40. This was later followed by both a general-audience overview in *The Atlantic* and a book, *Environment, Scarcity, and Violence* (Princeton University Press, 2001).

2 An excellent philosophical discussion of the nuances here can be found in Neil Levy, "Autonomy and Addiction," *Canadian Journal of Philosophy* 36, no. 3 (2006), 427–47, especially 432 and 431.

3 Andy Borowitz, "Trump Economic Plan Calls for Every American to Inherit Millions From Father," *New Yorker* (August 8, 2016); www.newyorker.com/humor/borowitz-report/trump-economic-plan-calls-for-every-american-to-inherit-millions-from-father (accessed September 16, 2016).

4 John Rawls, *A Theory of Justice* (Cambridge MA: Belknap Press, 1970). My characterization is crude but I hope not inaccurate. For further reflections on the basics of the theory and its relation to chance, see Mark Kingwell, "Throwing Dice: Luck of the Draw and the Democratic Ideal," *PhaenEx* 7, no. 1 (2012): 66–100; reprinted in Mark Kingwell, *Unruly Voices* (Windsor, Ontario: Biblioasis, 2012).

This is neither a matter of brute injustice in circumstances, nor a function of the (closely related) chances of who our parents are. In other words, Order-Three Risk is distinct from both Order-One and Order-Two Risk because it concerns individual orientation to risk in general. It is an independent personal relationship to chance that can, under certain circumstances, govern significant outcomes for other people.

How so? Well, imagine, once again, that we are in an original-choice position such as Rawls's thought-experiment. Some people might opt for unequal outcomes, on the chance that they would enjoy the fruits of inequality. They gamble on the benefits of unfair distribution working in their favor.

In this way, risk-tolerant participants in the choice game can skew results in favor of social rules that allow steep inequalities, with no welfare floor. These players may lose their gamble, of course; but meanwhile *everybody* loses because the game is skewed against fairness. And this is exactly what obtains in the so-called real world. Neo-liberal economics dominate life and choice, favoring the favored while maintaining a narrative of *possible* success for others - the American Dream or some similar bill of goods.

Once more, we could solve this problem by theoretically ruling aversion and tolerance out of the ideal situation. Attitude to risk (we might argue), in common with other personal factors such as height or physical beauty, must be excluded from one's self-knowledge under the conditions of ideal choice. This will clear the way for rational agreement about society's basic structure. But this move looks merely ad hoc, and therefore unjustified. More significantly, these behind-the-veil risk-positive people are just idealized cousins to the free-market risk-takers of the actual world, those who believe that they deserve larger outcomes because of what they have ventured. Such people don't believe they were born on third base; they believe they took a chance on a hanging off-speed pitch and hustled their way to that triple.

We can understand the significance of Order-Three Risk better by bringing it into even closer relation to the other two orders of risk. If risk-aversion and risk-tolerance are themselves part of the birthright lottery, not pure personal virtues, the game changes. Cheerleaders for 'entrepreneurship' and 'innovation' love to argue that risk-tolerance is an admirable cultivated quality, like courage or temperance (even if often ventured with other people's money). But what if it is more an inherited tendency and, as such, a morally vacuous feature, like height or beauty? This 'essential' quality of self might be just as much a matter of who your parents are as whether you were born in happy Denmark or benighted sub-Saharan Africa.

This in turn suggests that the distribution of attitude to risk–Order-Three Risk–demands justice consideration. We might need to *control for*, rather than merely assume, the uneven distributions of willingness to take chances. Indeed, if such distributions are having negative systemic effects at the widest level, reinforcing schemes of governance that favor risk tolerance, we should view regulation of Order-Three Risk as a central tenet of any just society. We can tolerate marginal gains scored by those who are physically attractive, or athletically blessed (Giselle Bündchen and Tom Brady are simply going to be better off than most people, given the world as we find it) but we would certainly not want such features to govern general outcomes of life chances for everyone. Risk-tolerance might be just as adventitious, and so just as irrelevant.

The political conclusion becomes ever-more obvious: risk is a matter for justice interventions at all conceptual levels. Loosening the sense of 'deserved' connection between personal qualities such as risk-tolerance and good outcomes is just as important as alleviating the consequences of Order-One Risk. Without both aspects, any attempt to realize justice concerning the consequences of birthright lottery will be hampered. Such attempts will fail to address the ongoing sense among the favored that they–and hence others–have what they have by right, and so that those less favored likewise deserve poor outcomes generated by the current arrangement.

In one clear and traditional sense, justice means to favor the unfavored, giving aid where it is called for. But perhaps to be more complete, justice also demands that we unfavor the favored. The core lesson is actually an old and familiar one, with new and renewed urgency. It is not enough to comfort the afflicted; we must also afflict the comfortable.

MEGA LOTTO

YOUR FUTURE'S JUST A CHANCE AWAY

A. 15°20 54 N 15°1223 E

B. 38 89 77°N 77 0365°W

C. 08°50 18 S 13°1404 E

D. 35°18 27 S 149°0729E

GET RICH. LIVE EASIER. NOW.

ANDREW ZOLLI

TOWARD A TRANSPARENT PLANET

Andrew Zolli oversees social, ecological, and humanitarian-impact programs at the satellite earth-imaging company Planet, Inc. He is the author (with Anne-Marie Healy) of *Resilience: Why Things Bounce Back* (2012), which examines how people and systems persist, recover, and thrive amid disruption. He also currently serves as the Chair of the Garrison Institute, an organization which explores the intersection between contemplative practice, systems science, and new modalities of social change. He was previously the creative and curatorial force behind the innovation and social change network PopTech, and has served as a Fellow of the National Geographic Society.

+ TECHNOLOGY, CONSERVATION, RESILIENCE THEORY

Tools not only shape what we can do, they shape what we can know. And in so doing, they not only accelerate scientific discovery, but *moral* discovery. From the alphabet to the telescope, from the internet to the gene sequencer, every new source of knowledge recasts human agency and thus, human responsibility. What was previously hidden becomes knowable; what is knowable becomes actionable; what is actionable becomes, eventually, ethically demanded. If, as Martin Luther King Jr said, the long arc of the moral universe bends toward justice, it is this cumulative weight of our knowledge, our expanding senses, and our ever-more truthful reckoning with the world that does the bending.

In this light, it is worth considering our current civilizational moment, one in which human beings are presented, simultaneously, with the most significant risks we have ever faced, and the greatest abundance of knowledge and capabilities we have ever possessed. We are now living through the early days of the Sixth Extinction: the sixth time in the 3.5 billion-year history of life on Earth that its biodiversity has collapsed, nearly taking the whole enterprise of life with it. It is a calamity of which we, through our transformation of the land, the oceans, and the atmosphere, are undoubtedly the cause. (In a school play about the extinction of the dinosaurs, we would be cast as the meteor.) This collapse in biodiversity is just one of several "planetary boundaries" that humanity has recently caused to be exceeded, in systems that are required for life to flourish on Earth. Unthinkingly, we are unweaving the world.

Yet we are also living, simultaneously, through a Second Renaissance, marked by an explosion of knowledge and capability that defies precedent and hyperbole. By one estimate, humanity is now producing about two-and-a-half million terabytes of data every day. The volume is growing so quickly that 90% of all accessible data on Earth was produced in the last two years alone – the byproduct of our relentless interrogation and subjugation of the world. We are, by all accounts, the most informed, capable, and (selectively) imperiled generation of human beings who have ever lived. We find ourselves in a collective footrace between our own dazzling ingenuity and existential risks of our own manufacture. Yet, by and large, we have barely calibrated the former to the latter.

Our problem is, first and foremost, a cognitive one. Human perception is exquisitely sensitized to changes that occur at roughly human scale, and at roughly human speeds. We are hyper-attentive to risks that are personified, and especially those presented to us in the form of simple parables. Our ability to notice change quickly collapses when things move much faster, or much slower than our preferred rate of perception. Likewise, we're generally blind to changes that happen at very large or very small scales, or to ones that occur outside our social world, in the background of our everyday awareness.

Alas, these are exactly the kind of changes–enormous, quiet, non-narrative, faceless, and often remote from our lived experiences–that are the hallmark of

Previous Page: Luuq, Somalia. A haven for hundreds of Somalia's "internally displaced persons," who live inside makeshift tents inside the oxbow.

the Anthropocene. The environmental writer Timothy Morton notes that this new age requires us to contend with what he calls "hyperobjects" – entities so vast in spatial or temporal scale that they exceed the usual dimensions of a human life. Such systems are so large and interconnected that they defeat traditional ideas about what a 'thing' is in the first place. Against such abstractions, our parochial hominid minds don't stand a chance – at least not on their own.

Thankfully, there are now technologies being developed that promise to help us sense these planetary changes, and transcribe them into the resonant frequencies of human cognition – to make change visible, accessible, and actionable. One organization developing such technologies is my own, a hybrid humanitarian/commercial enterprise called Planet (www.planet.com) which is deploying the largest constellation of Earth-observing satellites in history. Collectively, this system captures images of the entire surface of the Earth every day, at a resolution of three meters per pixel – the most detailed and comprehensive picture of the changing world ever recorded.

By collecting imagery everywhere, every day, Planet's satellites can watch events that were rarely, if ever, attended to: smallholder crops being grown in southeast Asia; refugee camps blooming in the Syrian desert; illegal deforestation occurring in the Peruvian Amazon, glaciers collapsing in Tibet; the pulsing growth of unplanned urban settlements in East Africa. Everywhere the system looks, we see change. And not just the signs of those that have occurred in the past, but the *precursors* of ones that might occur in the future: the subtle shifts in a crop growth that might suggest impending failure, or the illegal roads in a rainforest that often presage deforestation. Distributed quickly and widely to the right hands—not just corporations but communities, governments, and NGOs as well—this data can save lives, protect ecosystems, reduce suffering, build resilience, and improve human flourishing – enabling inclusive planetary stewardship.

An expansive "architecture of participation" is essential here – one rooted not just in providing wide access to information, but in developing the capacity and understanding of communities to use it well. Without these, powerful data simply supercharges a capable few at the expense of the many – widening, rather than narrowing inequality. When distributed appropriately, these tools help us collectively comprehend the complex and sometimes unintuitive ways in which our planet's systems, and our behaviors, are interconnected – and how an innocuous change in one area often correlates with a dramatic consequence in another. We are beginning to unravel how changes in land-use accelerate the risks of new pandemics; how a rural drought might shape the growth of nearby cities; or how overfishing in the oceans might cause an otherwise mysterious die-off on the land. As these observations and connections pile up, a new field, *planetary health*, is slowly emerging, which frames the health of ecosystems and people within an integrated whole.

One hopes that, as the resulting perspectival shift propagates through our culture, it also accelerates the possibility of a cultural and moral shift; a normative pivot in what we believe, and how we behave toward the Earth and its many living inhabitants. It's worth remembering that virtually all of human civilization, including our moral beliefs and values, our relationships and governance, our commerce and industry—*all* of it—evolved in the context of a relatively tranquil period on Earth, an interregnum between the end of the Paleolithic Ice Age, about 12 thousand years ago, and today. Our beliefs about the world, and our place within it, evolved in this nursery of stability and abundance, and it left its mark in our minds. The ideologies that won out in this period, rooted in the conquest of nature, in the possibility of limitless growth, and in our inherent separateness and superiority to other living things, *require* continued abundance and stability to underwrite and sustain them.

These ideologies will not survive unchallenged in an era of profound, planetary volatility, disruption, and risk. In their stead, we will have to recover the countervailing narrative, one in which the subject-object distinction falls away, and we understand ourselves as utterly enmeshed, and in deep solidarity with the larger community of life and the systems that support it. We're inventing the tools that can help us see this profound and simple truth, and rebuild our institutions and governance accordingly. Let's hope we grasp it in time.

ACTS OF GODS
[GEO]ENGINEERING RISK

RICHARD WELLER

Richard Weller is Professor and Chair of Landscape Architecture at the University of Pennsylvania where he also holds the Martin and Margy Meyerson Chair of Urbanism. Weller is author of five books on design and regional planning including *Boomtown 2050: Scenarios for a Rapidly Growing City* (2009) and *Made in Australia: The Future of Australian Cities* (2014). His recently published *Atlas for the End of the World* (2017) documents global flashpoints between urbanization and biodiversity.

+ GEOENGINEERING, CLIMATE SCIENCE, EARTH SCIENCE

The environmental activist Stuart Brand famously quipped of the Anthropocene that since we have now become gods we "have to get good at it."[1] But what does it mean to be a good god? For Brand, and his colleagues in the Breakthrough Institute with whom he penned the 2015 *Ecomodernist Manifesto*, it means creating a "good Anthropocene."[2] This, they say, "demands that humans use their growing social, economic, and technological powers to make life better for people, stabilize the climate, and protect the natural world."[3] The fulcrum of that statement–the thing upon which the fate of both people and the so-called natural world now depend–is a stable climate. And it is the probability that humanity will consciously attempt to engineer such stability that elevates us from our Holocene status as mere mortals to the good gods of the Anthropocene.

Technologies for geoengineering a stable climate are typically organized into two major categories: solar radiation management (SRM) and carbon dioxide removal (CDR). SRM technologies apply directly to the atmosphere (heaven), whereas CDR technologies apply directly to the land and the oceans (earth). Organized according to this dualistic divinity of heaven and earth, this article briefly summarizes and discusses the risks of both.

The Intergovernmental Panel on Climate Change stresses that stabilizing temperature increase to below two degrees Celsius, "will require an urgent and fundamental departure from business as usual." But as global population swells, the world urbanizes, and billions attempt to lift themselves out of poverty by whatever means possible, significant reductions in greenhouse gas emissions this century seem unlikely. Indeed, the European Union's Directorate-General for Climate Action has already concluded that the sum total of emission reduction measures proposed by the 189 individual nations who have prepared National Climate Plans under the (COP 21) Paris Agreement will not be enough to achieve the agreement's primary aim of holding carbon dioxide emissions below a two degree increase.

And even if we were to stop using fossil fuels today, the excess of carbon and other greenhouse gases already in the system means stabilization would not emerge of its own accord for some time. At their own immemorial rates, the geosphere, biosphere, hydrosphere and atmosphere, which together comprise the earth system, will absorb and adjust to our excesses and stable patterns will once again emerge; but by then the landscape in which global civilization is so deeply rooted will have shifted. As Harvard physicist and environmentalist David Keith writes, "carbon casts a long shadow onto the future: a thousand years after we stop pumping carbon into the air the warming will still be about half as large as it was on the day we stopped."

In the interim, climate instability is variously predicted to heighten both the intensity and frequency of destructive and deadly weather events which, in combination with

60 km —

Mesosphere

50 km —

40 km —

Ozone Layer

30 km —

Stratosphere

Proposed Stratospheric Veil

20 km —

10 km —

Troposphere

0 km —

50 km —

Lithosphere

100 km —

150 km —

200 km —

Asthenosphere

250 km —

inexorable sea level rise and temperature increase, will force the mass-migration of most species, inciting both political and ecological chaos. If those species, including humans, cannot adapt productively to these new conditions of instability, they will perish. Alternatively, in a bid to hold onto the world as we know it for a little longer, and buy some time to wean ourselves off fossil fuels once and for all, then stability—or what we may now recall fondly as Holocene weather—could, some think, be geoengineered.

As we know and trust them, engineers are especially risk averse professionals who design the world's mechanical structures and systems. Generally speaking they do so according to Newtonian physics with certitude regarding the performance and capacity of that which they make. Bridges span rivers, buildings stand up, and planes stay in the air. Geoengineers on the other hand propose to intervene directly in the workings of the earth system itself and for the first time in cosmological history they will attempt to reverse engineer an entire planet. A loose and unofficial collection of (overwhelmingly male) scientists and inventors, geoengineers are the vanguard of the Anthropocene, an epoch paradoxically defined (and confounded) by the fact that we have unwittingly and it seems very badly, already reengineered the planet.

SRM Heaven

Heavenly geoengineering concerns the control of global temperature through solar radiation management (SRM) and therefore addresses the symptoms rather than causes (carbon emissions) of anthropogenic climate change. Ideas for SRM include global dimming via orbiting sun-shades, increasing the earth's albedo by multiplying the density and brightness of clouds over the ocean, painting cities white, covering glaciers in white plastic and finally, the injection of sulfates (aerosols) into the stratosphere to deflect sunlight back into space. It is the latter, referred to as a 'veil,' that seems to rise to the top in cost-benefit and risk analyses and most consistently receive the imprimatur of prominent figures in the field.

Comprised of sulfuric acid suspended in tiny water droplets some 20 kilometers above the earth, the veil is relatively easy to manufacture. According to Keith, sulfur has "a near million to one" capacity to offset the effects of carbon dioxide. That is, one ton of sulfur suspended in the stratosphere deflecting sunlight back into space can offset the global warming effects of one million tons of carbon emissions. Because the sulfur falls to earth over the course of a year or so, the veil requires constant replenishment, which Keith has calculated at around one million tons per annum by the year 2070. And if that sounds frightening, bear in mind that humanity currently pumps around 50 million tons of sulfur dioxide as pollution into the lower atmosphere, killing around a million people every year. In any event, as its proponents are quick to point out, even if the act of loading sulfur into the earth system is not technically speaking reversible, the veil can always be lifted.

1 Stuart Brand, *Whole Earth Discipline* (London: Penguin, 2009) 1.

2 The Breakthrough Institute, "An Eco-Modernist Manifesto," http://www.ecomodernism.org (accessed December 27, 2016).

3 Ibid.

4 Rajendra K. Pachauri, *Climate Change 2014: Synthesis Report. Contribution of Working Groups I, II, and III to the Fifth Assessment Report of the Intergovernmental Panel on Climate Change* (Geneva: IPCC, 2014). Available at http://www.ipcc.ch/pdf/assessment-report/ar5/syr/SYR_AR5_FINAL_full_wcover.pdf.

5 European Commission, "Questions and Answers on the Paris Agreement," http://ec.europa.eu/clima/policies/international/negotiations/paris/docs/qa_paris_agreement_en.pdf (accessed June 1, 2016).

6 David Keith, *A Case for Climate Engineering* (Cambridge: MIT Press, 2013), 29.

7 Ibid., 6.

8 Ibid., 252.

9 Ibid., 70.

10 Ibid., 60.

11 Ibid., 16.

12 Dale Jamieson, "Ethics and Intentional Climate Change," *Climatic Change* 33, no. 3 (1996): 323–36.

13 Christopher J. Preston (ed.), *Engineering the Climate: The Ethics of Solar Radiation Management* (London: Lexington Books, 2014), 6.

14 Keith, *A Case for Climate Engineering*, 11.

15 Oliver Morton, *The Planet Remade: How Geoengineering Could Change the World* (New Jersey: Princeton University Press, 2015), 372–73.

16 Ibid.

17 See Mike Hume, *Can Science Fix Climate Change: A Case Against Climate Engineering* (Oxford: Polity Press, 2014); Clive Hamilton, *Earthmasters: The Dawn of the Age of Climate Engineering* (New Haven: Yale University Press, 2013).

18 Mike Hulme, "Reducing the Future to Climate," in Libby Robin, Sverker Sorlin & Paul Warde (eds), *The Future of Nature: Documents of Global Change* (New Haven: Yale University Press, 2013), 518.

19 Clive Hamilton, "*The Anthropocene as Rupture*," *The Anthropocene Review* 3, no. 2 (2016).

By diffracting sunlight back into space the great promise of the veil is that it could quickly reduce global temperature, forestall arctic sea-ice melt, and save communities and estuarine ecosystems from imminent sea-level rise. Stabilized or reduced temperatures also hold the prospect of avoiding predicted crop losses associated with global warming. Keith and other geoengineering heavyweights, such as Ken Caldeira from the Department of Global Ecology at Stanford, variously suggest that food supply in Africa and India could significantly increase by virtue of geoengineering. Keith concludes that even though a stratospheric veil cannot reduce the risk of humanity's transfer of carbon from underground reservoirs to the atmosphere "[i]t's hard to overstate the importance of geoengineering's ability to reduce risk for current generations as there are no other methods that can reduce these risks significantly in the next half century."

So what's the problem?

In 1996 Dale Jamieson, Professor of Environmental Studies and Philosophy at New York University, set out four standards that any geoengineering proposal must meet: they must be technically feasible, must have predictable consequence, must produce economic states preferable to the alternatives and, finally, must not violate any "well founded" ethical principles. These principles include democratic decision-making, avoiding irreversible change, and "learning to live with nature." Christopher Preston, Professor of Ethics at the University of Montana, claims that, to date, no geoengineering project has met these standards.

A stratospheric veil is technically feasible but predictions of its consequences range from potentially stopping the monsoon and putting more than a billion people at risk of starvation, to "a best guess" that it will "reduce the damage from climate change in most regions" but "make some regions worse off – perhaps by increasing drought." Sulfur particles may also damage the ozone layer and as they fall to earth they will compound pollution-related health problems and further acidify the oceans. Former editor of Nature Oliver Morton points out that the veil may also work too well and by cooling the planet, begin a new ice age.

Of course a veil would be constantly monitored and could be adjusted, but this leads perhaps to its biggest problem: the question how it would be regulated. Who sets the temperature? What of rogue states and military applications? And would it not be blamed for all the catastrophes we used to 'write off' as acts of God? Finally, as to the violation of the "well founded" ethical principle of "learning to live with nature," who is to say what this means when the nature of the Anthropocene is itself a cultural construct?

Whilst recognizing that the advent of geoengineering "changes what it is for humans to be humans and what it is for nature to be nature" and that for some it "takes human empire over the border of blasphemy," Morton goes so far as to discuss geoengineering as potentially a thing of beauty. He suggests that it could manifest a new understanding of nature as a co-evolutionary process, not a separate ahistorical thing. On the other hand, prominent critics such as Mike Hulme and Clive Hamilton, consider any such techno-fix to climate change a perpetuation of the pathological modernity that got us into this predicament in the first place. Such fixes, they argue, will have the negative effect of reinforcing the status quo. Hulme rails against geoengineering as a form of climate determinism arguing that it is "nurtured by elements of a Western cultural pessimism that promote the pathologies of vulnerability, fatalism, and fear" and that reducing climate change to a technical problem is stifling the "human creativity, imagination and ingenuity [that] will create radically different social, cultural and poltical worlds in the future." Similarly, for Hamilton climate change is not just an engineering problem, and nor is it just a continuation of cultural and environmental history; it is, as he puts it, "a rupture" requiring far more radical revisions of what it means to be human and, along with it, the fundamental reorganization of society.

But if it is true that due to the loading of carbon since at least the late 18th century the climate is already a reengineered system, and one that will negatively impact the lives of many of the world's most vulnerable, then such philosophical critique at this point in time seems like sophistry. The conundrum of climate change is that we are damned if we do and damned if we don't. The most compelling argument for stabilizing temperature with a stratospheric veil is that it would buy us time: time for better research, time for energy transition, and time for spatial, political, *and* philosophical adaptation to this new reality.

CDR Earth

Geoengineering the heavens concerns temperature stabilization therefore it only addresses the thermal symptoms, not the causes of anthropogenic climate change. To broach the direct cause–that is, the excess of carbon in the earth system–we need to come down to earth and consider carbon dioxide removal (CDR) proposals.

Proposed methods for 'mopping up' excess carbon in the earth system include adding iron to the oceans to cause phytoplankton blooms, converting agricultural waste to bio-char before it decomposes and releases carbon, filtering carbon from industrial outlets, speeding up what trees do by mechanical carbon capture from the air, and establishing vast forests to 'naturally' sequester carbon. Apart from chemically manipulating the oceans, which is akin to manipulating the stratosphere, all these ideas are relatively low-risk and may all, therefore, have a role to play. Here, however, I focus on carbon sequestration through forestry and relate it to other land use pressures that will shape the global landscape this century.

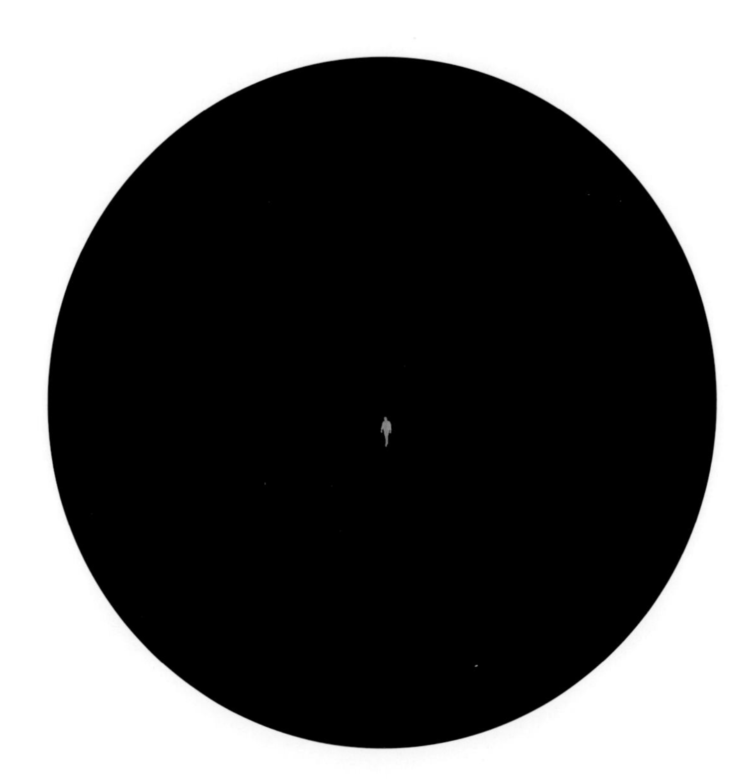

Land clearance for agriculture and urban growth is one of the biggest contributors to carbon emissions. As global populations urbanize and more people shift toward high-protein diets, more land must be cleared for crops and livestock. Humanity extracts one-third of its protein from livestock: this requires 3.38 billion hectares (38%) of the earth's ice-free land in order to graze and produce the feed crops necessary to sustain livestock. It is the largest single land use on the planet. Livestock then erode and compact soil, pollute water with nitrous oxide and ammonia, and expel 37% of all methane into the atmosphere. High crop yields are only made possible through the liberal application of industrially manufactured fertilizers and pesticides, themselves drawn from fossil fuels and expelling carbon in the (Haber-Bosch) process of their production. Most problematic is that reactive nitrogen run-off from industrialized agriculture causes extensive eutrophication of inland waterways and the proliferation of 'dead' (hypoxic) zones in the oceans. If carbon weren't the hot issue, nitrogen would be.

In 1990 the world had 4,128 million hectares of forest; by 2015 this area has decreased to 3,999 million hectares. According to the 2015 Soil Atlas, around 13 million hectares of forest are cleared every year, and of the world's primary forests around 40 million hectares have disappeared since 2000. Naturally occurring forests are in decline, planted forests are increasing. Though not always the case, forested lands are generally increasing in rich countries and decreasing in poor countries. Before modern agriculture, tropical rainforests covered about 1.6 billion hectares of the earth's surface. In his 2015 report to the Club of Rome on the state of the world's rainforests, Claude Martin estimates that one-half has been eradicated due to agriculture, logging, and mining, much of this occurring in the last few decades. A further one-quarter of the world's rainforests is, according to Martin, degraded. It is currently estimated that 4.9 million hectares of rainforest are lost each year. At this rate the earth's entire

Above: An average American produces 21.55 metric tons (47,510 lbs) of CO2 equivalents a year. In contrast a single (average) tree can sequester 2.8 metric tons of CO2 per year.

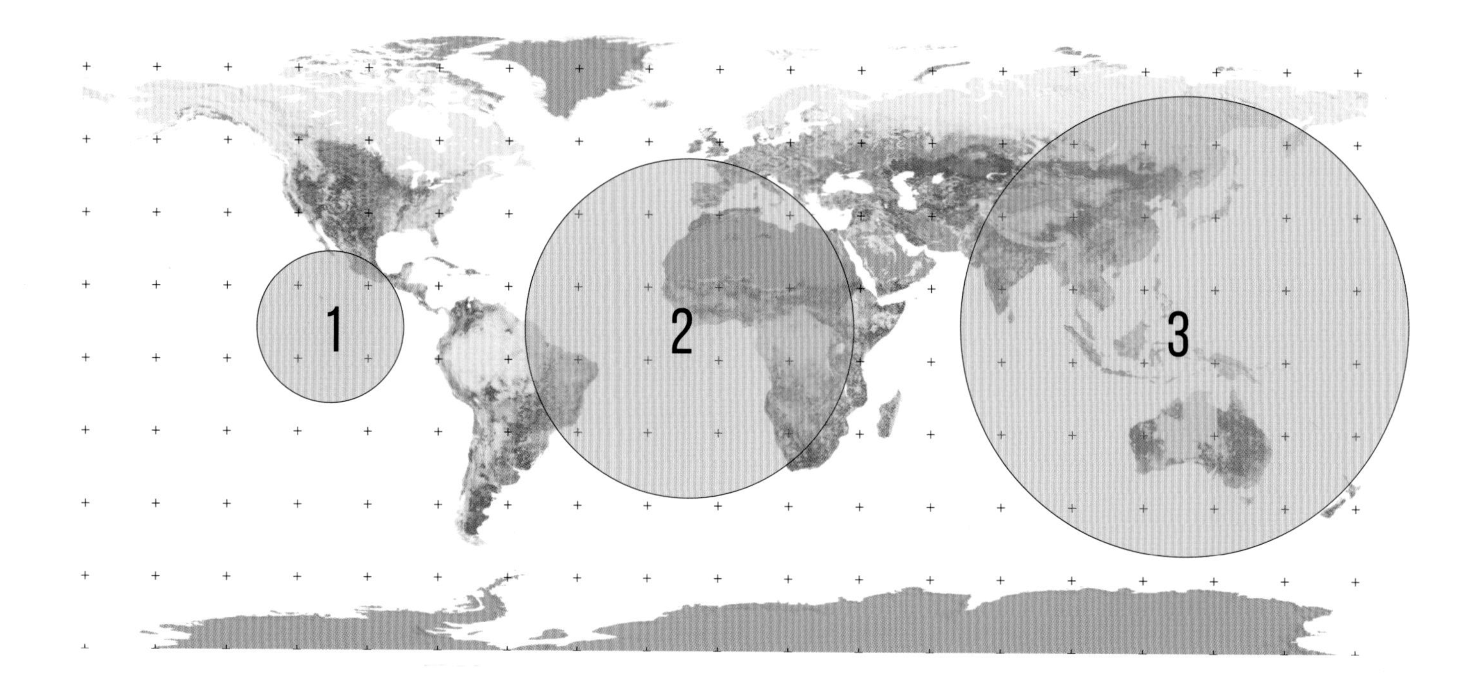

rainforest biome–exempting the 9.8% (at 2008) under protection–will be eradicated in a little over 100 years from now. To do this would be to radically destabilize an already volatile earth system and sacrifice life's most prodigious biodiversity before it is barely documented. In return 'we' will get relatively small quantities of palm oil, soy beans, cocoa, and beef.

Against this trend of deforestation, the Paris Agreement urges the retention of existing carbon sinks (vegetated landscapes), which, if taken seriously, bodes well for the world's ecoregions and will encourage reforestation in accordance with Aichi target 15 of the United Nations' Convention on Biological Diversity. Target 15 states that "by 2020, ecosystem resilience and the contribution of biodiversity to carbon stocks has been enhanced, through conservation and restoration, including restoration of at least 15 per cent of degraded ecosystems, thereby contributing to climate change mitigation and adaptation and to combating desertification."

According to Morton there are about five billion tons of excess carbon in the earth system per year. If that carbon was to be sequestered through forestry, he concludes that it would require a forest of approximately seven million square kilometers. Morton doesn't explain how he reached this figure but if a single tree absorbs around 20 kilograms of carbon per year then 250 billion trees would be needed to sequester the five billion tons of excess carbon in the system. If those trees were planted on 10-meter centers, the forest would have a density of 31,250 trees per square kilometer, adding up to eight million square kilometers of new forest, about two-and-a-half times the size of India.

Above: (1) The world's current crop land. (2) The world's entire supply of arable land. (3) The land area required for food production for a global population consuming at the rate of average Americans (1.4 hectares per person).

Right: A forest the size of 2.5 Indias would be required to sequester the world's current excess of five billion tons of carbon per year.

To consider the feasibility of such a forest, we must first find space for it in the Earth's total ice-free terrestrial area of 149,000,000 km2. First, we have to discount the 39,000,000 km2 of the world's existing forest, then 15,000,000 km2 of current crop land and 33,000,000 km2 of current grazing land. Further, we should also subtract

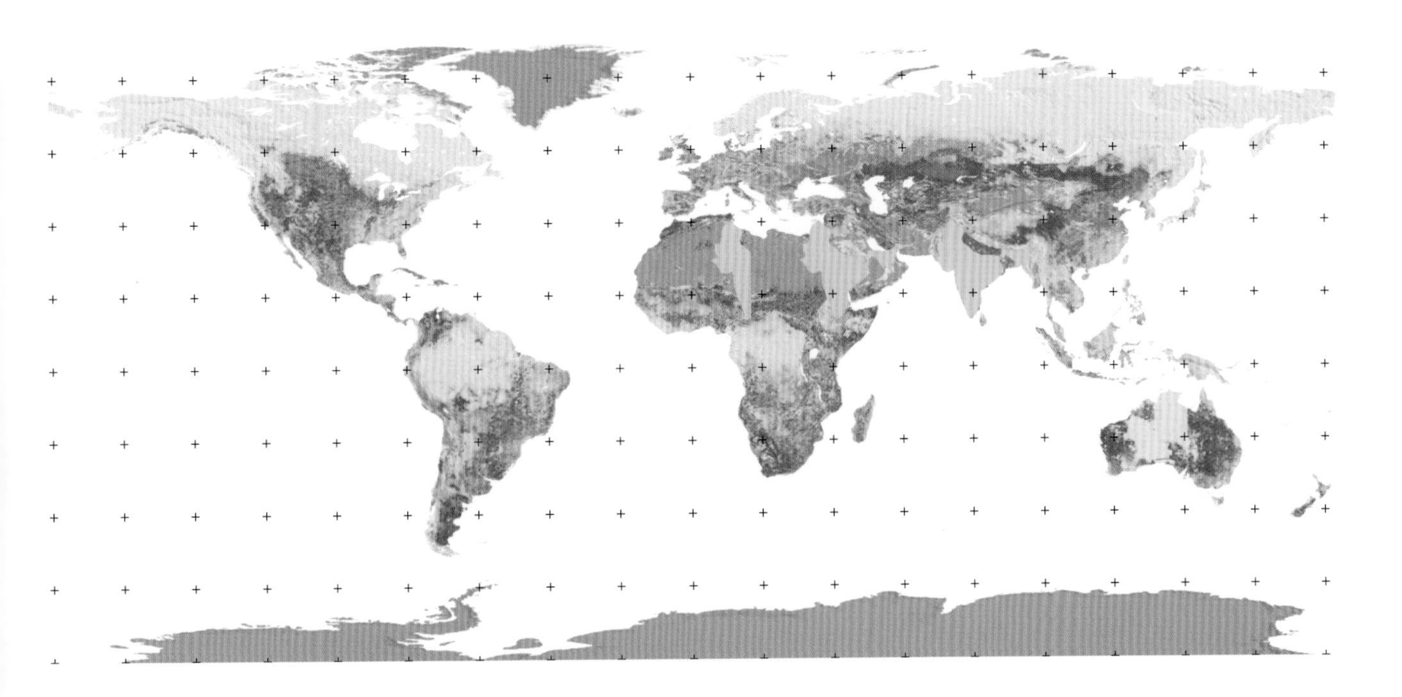

the 26,000,000 km2 of potentially arable land which is not yet, but surely will be farmed if we are to feed a global population of 10 billion by 2100. This leaves a total of 36,000,000 km2 on which to develop our sequestration forest. The problem is, however, that 33% (49,000,000 km2) of the earth's terrestrial surface is desert – by definition land unsuited to forestry.

In this scenario, to complement the heavenly work of creating the veil, the earthly task becomes a matter of greening the deserts. It is important to note, however, that the performance of such a forest in the totality of the earth system is not at all well understood and therefore the true calculation of its size is the stuff of conjecture. For example, a complicating factor is that when carbon is sucked out of the atmosphere, as such a massive forest would certainly do, the oceans react proportionally by giving up more carbon. Morton, for one, concludes that "there are undoubtedly ways to encourage the storage of carbon in the biosphere through soil management, agronomy, and forestry... [b]ut such actions do not store carbon on the scale needed to put a serious dent in the fossil-fuel-driven trajectory of atmospheric carbon dioxide."

In addition to tensions between the expansion of the global food bowl and sequestration forestry the major impact on the earth system is the unprecedented scale and pace of urbanization. In 2015 the global population was estimated at 7.3 billion people. The United Nations forecasts that this will grow to 8.5 billion by 2030, 9.7 billion by 2050, and anywhere up to 13.3 billion by 2100. Given these forecasts and the rate at which the world is urbanizing it seems reasonable to expect something in the order of at least an additional three billion people living in cities this century. To facilitate this means the equivalent of 464 New York Cities are required. In terms of sheer construction, this means building 5.5 New Yorks per year between now and 2100. Because building entirely new cities in new locations is expensive, and because existing cities tend to resist densification, we can expect much of this new global development to be what is pejoratively known as sprawl. Supplying energy, food,

20 Phytoplankton construct themselves in part from carbon and upon their death fall to the ocean floor where their remains are absorbed into the carbonate rock cycle.

21 Future Directions International, "The Future Prospects for Global Arable Land," http://www.futuredirections.org.au/publication/the-future-prospects-for-global-arable-land/ (accessed June 24, 2016).

22 Food and Agriculture Organization of the United Nations, "Livestock's Long Shadow: Environmental Issues and Options" (Rome: 2006). Available at http://www.fao.org/docrep/010/a0701e/a0701e00.HTM.

23 Christine Chemnitz & Jes Weigelt (eds), *The Soil Atlas 2015* (Berlin: Heinrich Böil Foundation & Institute for Advanced Sustainability Studies, 2015), 15. Available at http://globalsoilweek.org/wp-content/uploads/2014/12/soilatlas2015_web_141221.pdf.

24 Claude Martin, *On the Edge: The State and Fate of the World's Tropical Rainforests*, Report to the Club of Rome (Vancouver: Greystone Books, 2015).

25 Toby A. Gardner, et al., "Prospects for Tropical Forest Biodiversity in a Human-Modified World," *Ecology Letters* 12, no. 6 (2009): 561–82.

26 S. Vaughan, *The State and Fate of Tropical Forests* (Winnipeg: International Institute for Sustainable Development, 2015). Available at http://www.iisd.org/sites/default/files/publications/state-fate-tropical-rainforests-commentary.pdf.

27 Convention on Biological Diversity, "Aichi Biodiversity Targets," https://www.cbd.int/sp/targets/ (accessed September 10, 2016).

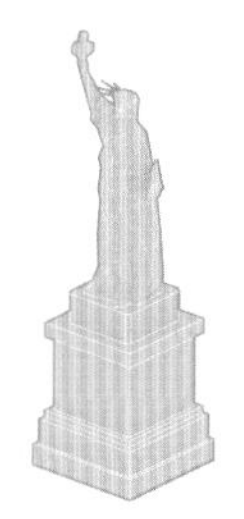

X 357

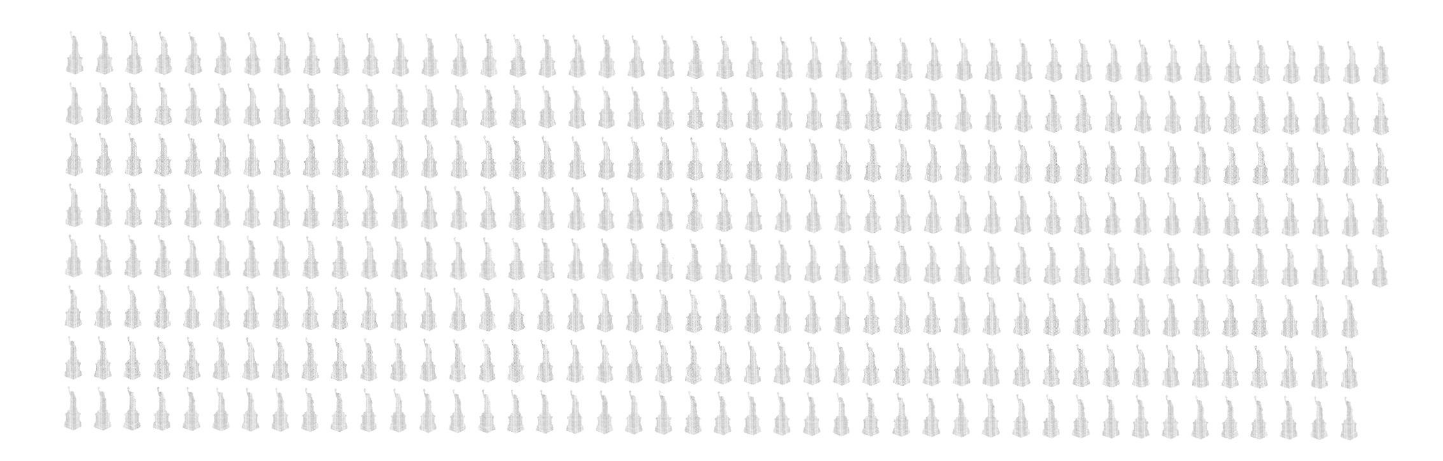

28 Morton, *The Planet Remade*, 258.

29 NC State University College of Agriculture & Life Sciences, "Tree Facts," http://www.ncsu.edu/project/treesofstrength/treefact.htm [accessed December 1, 2016]; Sarah Moos, "50,000 Trees," *Scenario 04:* Building the Urban Forest (2014), http://scenariojournal.com/article/50000-trees/.

30 Although this grazing land has some tree cover, it is not at the density required to meet the sequestration demand.

31 Morton, *The Planet Remade*, 262.

32 United Nations, Department of Economic and Social Affairs, Population Division, *World Population Prospects: The 2015 Revision, Key Findings and Advance Tables* (2015). Available at https://esa.un.org/unpd/wpp/Publications/.

33 Neil Brenner & Christian Schmid, *"Planetary Urbanization,"* in Matthew Gandy (ed.), Urban Constellations (Berlin: Jovis Verlag, 2011), 12.

Right: A world of 10 billion people living at the material standard of today's average American would produce 216 billion metric tons of CO2.

water, and housing (not to mention the consumer pleasures of late capitalism) for so many additional people will need to be carefully designed so as not put the earth system at further risk of irreversible failure.

The UN reports that there is a 23% chance that global population will stabilize or fall before 2100. This would bring to an end a growth cycle which began when a global population of around four million nomads started to transition into settlements with the birth of the agricultural revolution. The critical question is what shape the earth system will be in by the time peak population is reached. Along with the Milankovitch cycles (the angular orbit of the earth in relation to the sun), the climate is affected by the chemical constituency of and interrelationships between the atmosphere, the oceans, and the land. The world's oceans and forests act as planetary lungs breathing carbon in and oxygen out: they distribute heat, water, and nutrients (indeed all the elements of the periodic table) via vast interwoven convection currents driven by incoming sunlight and the differential between the tropics and the poles. Understanding and being able to predictively model the dynamics of this planetary metabolism, and how "planetary urbanism" impacts it, is the future of geoengineering. It is also the future of humanity.

While landscape architects can't do much about the heavens, as intermediaries between the arts and sciences and between development and ecology, they can surely play a role here on earth. There is a vast landscape of risk before us.

Mt. Carbon 52,500 m

Mt. Everest 8,848 m

KRISTINA HILL

RISK, UNCERTAINTY +

RAPID SEA

THE INEVITABILITY OF

LEVEL RISE

Kristina Hill develops adaptation strategies for sea level rise, focusing on design innovations, hydrology, and social justice. She helped to develop a new water strategy for New Orleans in 2013, and recently edited the 100th anniversary issue of the Ecological Society of America's journal, *Frontiers*, on infrastructure for adaptation to climate change. She received her PhD from Harvard University, and is an associate professor at UC Berkeley in landscape architecture and environmental planning.

+ PLANNING, TECHNOLOGY, RESILIENCE THEORY

In April, I opened an email from the director of a regional agency that regulates development in a big chunk of the San Francisco Bay shore-zone. He had just heard a well-known federal official state that sea level rise would be in the range of six to nine feet by the year 2060.[1] In response to this, the director told me that plans to restore tidal wetlands for storm protection no longer made sense, saying "that's it, we'll have to build walls now." As it turned out, the estimate was the personal opinion of the official – not new data, as her audience had understood. But her statement changed San Francisco Bay's regional conversation, pushing it towards thinking of walls as the answer to sea level rise, when in fact walls are neither the only nor the best option, no matter how terrifying the numbers for sea level rise become.

Risk is often described as an intentional interaction with uncertainty.[2] People engaged in planning for coastal areas are intentionally interacting with uncertainties – not about whether the sea will rise, but about how high, when, and whether a specific strategy for coping will work as planned. Each new report about melting ice sheets and shallow groundwater raises the risk that the strategies we are beginning to discuss now will be inadequate, or that we will begin to implement them too late.[3]

San Francisco Bay has about a thousand miles of shoreline.[4] Coastal land values have risen rapidly over the past three decades as shoreline industries and military bases have mostly disappeared, and water quality has improved.[5] Extremely high levels of investment in housing markets, together with voters' resistance to up-zoning, are putting pressure on every piece of open land that isn't protected from development by law, especially parcels with water views. For example, 8–10,000 units of new housing have been approved for construction on a flat, artificial island where most of the land lies only three feet above current sea levels.[6] Regional highways and rail lines that are critical to the economy of the region hug the Bay shore, as do airports, landfills, and sewage treatment plants. The Pacific Institute has estimated that just half-a-meter of sea level rise would expose more than 150,000 people, 140 contaminated sites, 1,000 miles of roads, both major airports, and eight major wastewater treatment plants to flooding.[7]

At the same time, the region has been in the process of restoring tens of thousands of acres of tidal wetlands that were lost to urban land filling, agriculture, and industrial-scale salt harvesting. The Bay is a muddy waterbody, thanks to sediments that flowed into it from extensive gold mining in the Sierras during the 19th century. That silt protects the Bay from harmful algal blooms by blocking sunlight from penetrating the water, but it also makes it harder to observe some of the interactions among plants, animals, and artificial structures that could be used for adaptation to higher sea levels. For instance, I work with underwater drones to track the arrival of warmer-water species like the California sea hare in shallow arms of the Bay. The drone cameras are often blinded by the silt, forced to rely on sensing instruments instead of visible light. But this silt can also be collected and piled into berms to allow incoming tides to re-build and elevate the surfaces of wetlands. Without adding silt, these extensive wetlands will eventually collapse as tidal waters deepen above them, taking the nursery function they provide for fish and shellfish with them. Wetlands and submerged seagrass meadows are a critical foundation for the Bay's ecosystems, and under normal conditions they would migrate landward as the seas rise. But in an urbanized Bay Area, they can't migrate. Wetlands are blocked from moving upland at the edge of cities by levees and riprap, left to shrink by erosion and collapse in deeper tides.

Most environmental organizations see new housing along the coast as a threat to habitat goals, and talk about sea level rise as a reason to stop development. They want to remove low-lying urban areas and allow wetlands to migrate inland, both as a flood protection measure for urban areas and as a way of maintaining the ecosystems themselves.[8] A small parcel property tax was recently passed across all nine counties that touch the Bay, supporting wetland construction. The Bay Area is arguably the first major urban region to vote in favor of using new property taxes to build a landscape armature to protect against sea level rise. But thanks to pressure from housing markets and inaction by governments, new and relatively unprotected high-end development projects are being built that increase the region's exposure to losses from flooding. Each new building also adds urgency to property owners' demands for walls on the current shoreline, which would build the urban edge into a drastically more permanent and expensive barrier against the influx of tides and their wetland ecosystems. Pressure is essentially building from both the land side and the water side, and concrete walls filled with steel rebar would be a physical expression of the unresolved conflict between risks and needs.

Design has a long history of taking risks at the shoreline. We develop strategies to interact with uncertainty like chess players, informed by experience and a sense of pattern. In ancient Mediterranean cities, people built walls of rock stacked in the water along steep, rocky coasts to protect their navies and merchant fleets from storms. They extended those walls into building harbor sequences to control the movement of goods and people with gates. The contemporary version of this can be seen in the large, dynamic floodgates of cities like Rotterdam and London. An alternate design history was documented by Pliny the Elder around 30 AD, when he served as a Roman soldier along what is now the northern Dutch and German coast. He described people living on artificial sand mounds (terps), that provided a retreat from coastal storm floods. These mounds evolved into linear dikes and canals, becoming a system of landforms used historically by the Dutch to live in a submerging coastal landscape. While most of these landforms were designed to be static, the new Zandmotor–an artificial sand spit designed to erode as waves take its sand to widen the beaches north of Rotterdam–represents a contemporary version of intentionally dynamic landforms.

As these examples have shown, building walls is not always the best outcome: in some places, dynamic landscape armatures work better. To help expand our awareness of options for adapting to higher sea levels, I developed a simple four-quadrant diagram that maps a 'solution space' instead of a Cartesian one. It is defined by two axes: the first represents the percentage of landform that exists or is proposed for a given section of coastline; the second represents the percentage of walls that exist or are proposed along that same coastline. Together, they form four quadrants representing dynamic walls and static walls, or dynamic landforms and static landforms. It can be used to force a broader conversation about options, before people rush to propose dynamic walls (e.g., tidegates, surge barriers) or static landforms (e.g., levees and mounds made of fill).

This coastal strategies diagram can represent existing conditions around the entire San Francisco Bay, or show them city-by-city, or parcel-by-parcel. Like an altimeter guiding a pilot, the diagram can be used iteratively over decades to track evolving conditions, as well as proposed adaptations along the edge of the Bay. It allows planners and designers to ask, where might walls be appropriate, and how many? One of the insights we gained using the diagram to guide interdisciplinary conversations is that it is common for walls to be more expensive to replace than landforms, since the footings and relieving platforms associated with seawalls must often be excavated and replaced as well. That suggests that future generations will thank us if the diagram quadrants for 'walls' are relatively empty.

The other major insight we've gained so far is that treating the shore-zone as a line–along which all the work of protection and adaptation has to happen–creates unnecessary conceptual and strategic limits. A wall must be very large to provide

1 These remarks were reported on by Don Jergler, "Sea Level Rise Will Be Worse and Come Sooner," *Insurance Journal* (April 12, 2016).

2 After the North Sea flood of 1953 killed more than 1800 people in the Netherlands, planners began to define risk explicitly as the degree of exposure (usually defined in terms of property value) multiplied by the probability of an event. American planners adopted this approach for planning nuclear facilities in the 1970s, and many risk assessment professionals now consider this the only appropriate definition of risk for planning and design.

3 See for example, R.M. DeConto & D. Pollard, "Contribution of Antarctica to Past and Future Sea-level Rise," *Nature* 531, no. 7596 (2016): 591–97.

4 By way of comparison, researchers at the Virginia Institute of Marine Sciences have estimated that the Chesapeake Bay has a tidal shoreline approximately 11,000 miles long. The coast of the Hawaiian Islands has been estimated at about 1,000 miles and Alaska's coastline at 33,000 miles.

5 This is a common pattern for many urban areas, described in greater detail in Kristina Hill, "Climate-Resilient Urban Waterfronts," in Jeroen Aerts, et al. (eds), *Climate Adaptation and Flood Risk in Coastal Cities* (Amsterdam: Earthscan Climate, 2011).

6 Dealing with sea level rise so far has involved building new multi-story structures on plinths of fill, three to six feet above current elevations: Kevin Stark, et al., "Major S.F. Bayfront Developments Advance Despite Sea Rise Warnings," *SFPublicPress.org* (July 29, 2015), http://sfpublicpress.org/news/searise/2015-07/major-sf-bayfront-developments-advance-despite-sea-rise-warnings.

7 M. Heberger et al., "Potential Impacts of Increased Coastal Flooding in California Due to Sea-level Rise," *Climatic Change* 109 (2011): 229–49.

8 The Baylands Habitat Goals Scientific Update was completed in 2015, http://baylandsgoals.org/ (accessed August 27, 2016).

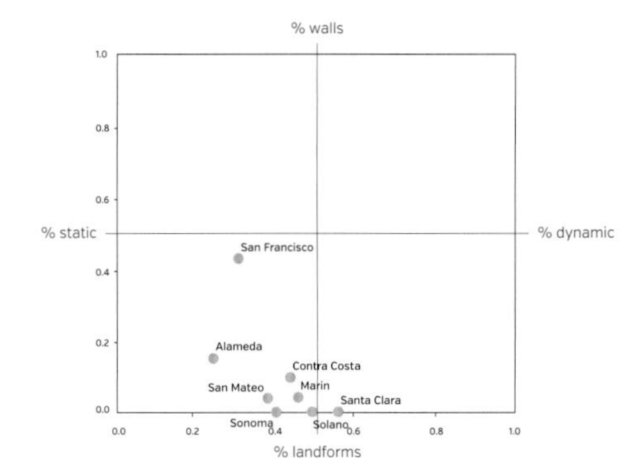

Above: Status of the San Francisco Bay shoreline by county (2016). San Francisco County has the highest percentage of walls along its shore, while Santa Clara County has the highest precentage of wetlands.

OPENROV
COCKPIT
Hold:
Depth
Heading
26.7
0.540A
9.2v

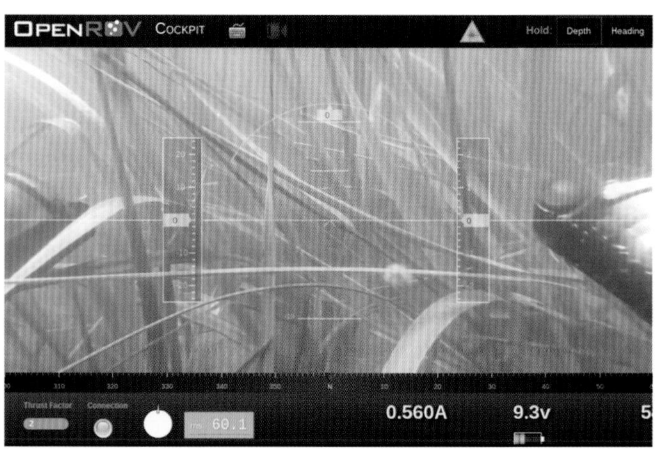
OPENROV
COCKPIT
Hold:
Depth
Heading
60.1
0.560A
9.3v

OPENROV

the protection needed for a fragile urban district that would be damaged, or create hazards for humans, in even temporary floods. As we learned in New Orleans, walls are brittle and prone to sudden, catastrophic failures that can kill. Large landscape armatures–made of dunes and beaches and wetlands, as well as dikes and mounds–can be overtopped without failing. But the urban districts they are paired with must then be resilient to temporary flooding, or better yet, be adapted to permanent flooding from high water tables or river water. The insight is that the type of coastal design we choose should be paired with a robust urban district design.

In Rotterdam's Nesselande district, luxury single-family homes were built on pile foundations over ponds formed by a high groundwater table. People live right on top of the water that could otherwise flood their homes. The new homes were intended to reduce market pressures on existing homes, in an effort to maintain income diversity in the district. The pond forms are at once delicate and robust, like living suspended over a mirror made of water. Housing in Hamburg's Hafencity is built on mounded plinths between canals, making it safe to occupy during annual flood events. The aesthetic experiences of these districts allow people to see the dynamics of their world, embracing change with a combination of poignancy, beauty, and risk that might be called a climate change sublime.

I can imagine a San Francisco Bay where adaptive urban districts, assembled in and over permanently high water tables and crisscrossed by canals, are protected and connected by braids of landscape in a honeycomb pattern of micro-polders. Some polders would contain mixed-use districts or corporate campuses, others would be reserved for habitat or recreation or sewage plants. This honeycomb pattern could even be built in what is now Bay shallow water, protecting existing development; or it could be built in areas that will be flooded by groundwater 30 years from now, making traditional roads and buildings obsolete. The absence of hurricane storm surges would allow this region to build tiered development right to the edge of a new Bay level, incorporating acceptable levels of risk. That's the vision I'm working with local agencies to share, gradually incorporating and addressing the concerns about risk that arise, trying to align the interests of developers, elected officials, housing activists, and conservationists.

But as a professional thinker and teacher, I know that there are additional risks introduced by the scale of global climate change. We know very little about the implications of multiple sea level rise crises occurring simultaneously around the entire world. What will happen to commodity prices for materials we need to adapt? Will global financial markets make borrowing money for adaptation too expensive, because every major coastal city is trying to borrow at the same time? I can only speculate that regions where adaptation investments happen sooner will be better off, since waiting makes it more likely that local efforts will be overtaken by regional and national or even international events.

Since the San Francisco region lacks hurricanes, federal financial support for adaptation is unlikely. The Bay Area will need to find ways of adapting with the help of private housing markets and international capital. But the goal of encouraging private developers to build adaptive urban districts is almost impossible to achieve without leadership from the public sector to, literally, lay the groundwork for new districts that are designed to function with permanently higher water levels. If there is a way for private sector corporations to profit from building floodable development, and contribute to adding an armature of protective coastal landscapes, California's cities by the Bay had better find it fast. Once everyone sees the water rising, the smarter investments may be elsewhere.

RETRENCH

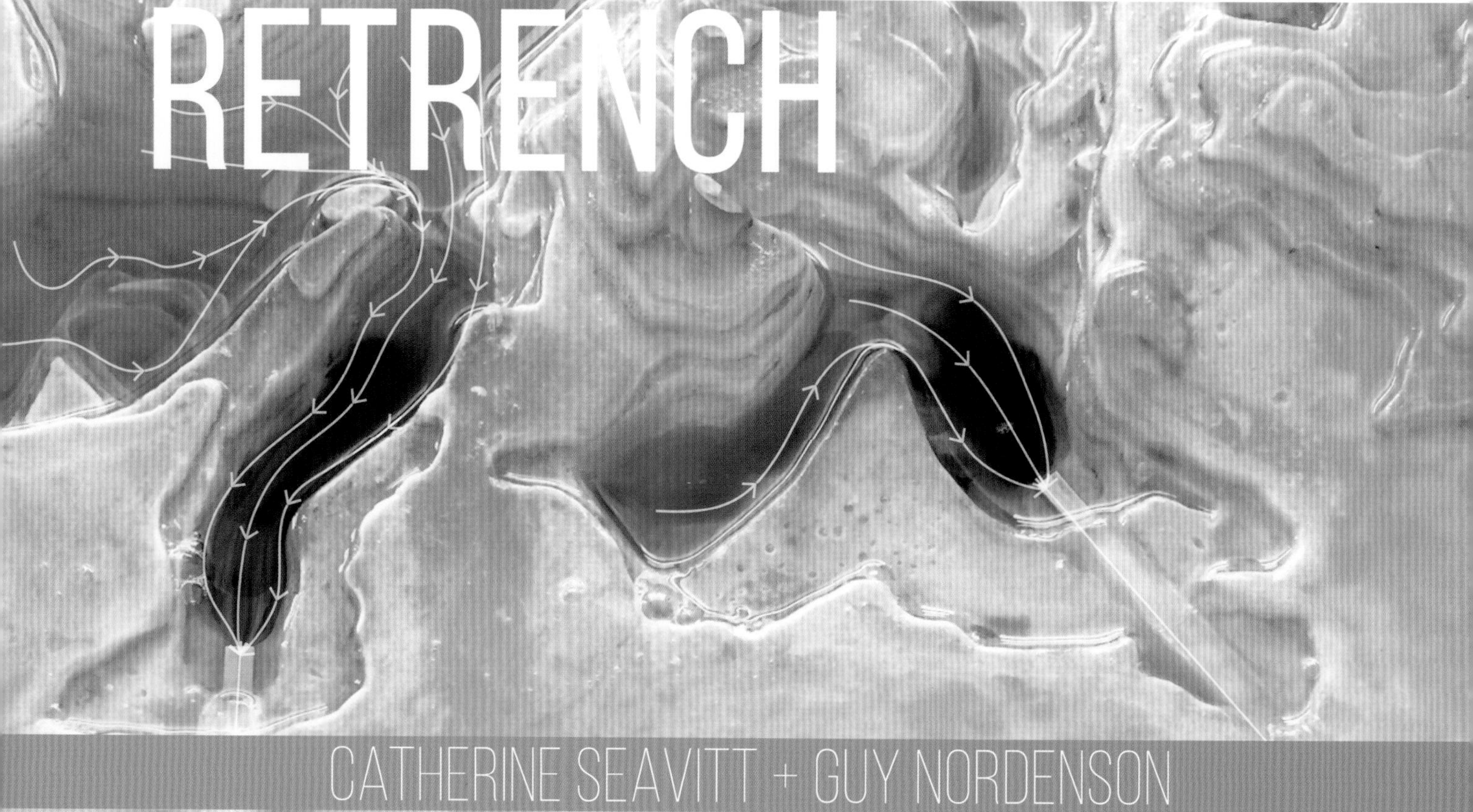

CATHERINE SEAVITT + GUY NORDENSON

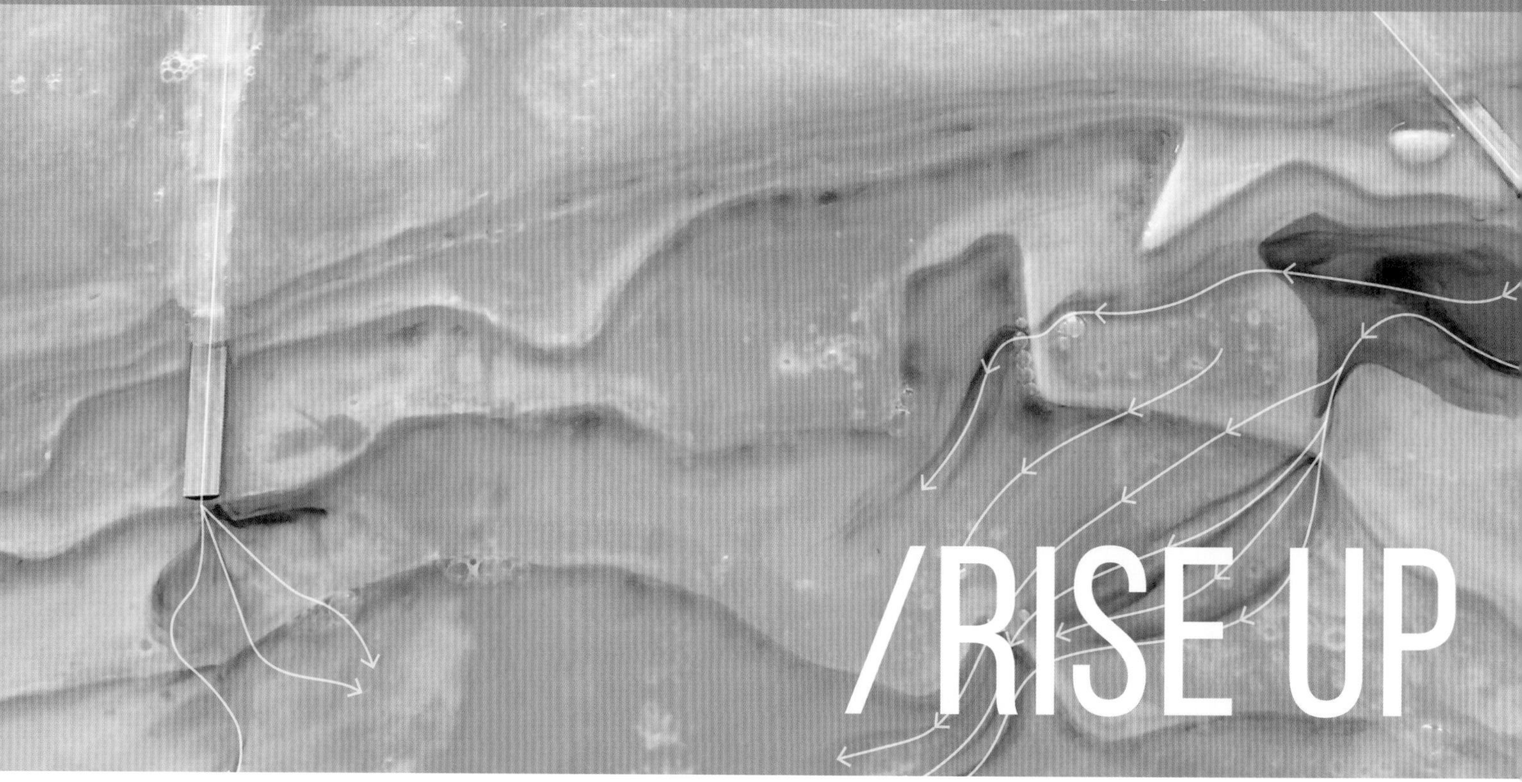

/RISE UP

Catherine Seavitt is Associate Professor of Landscape Architecture at the City College of New York and principal of Catherine Seavitt Studio. Her design research at Jamaica Bay, New York, as part of the Structures of Coastal Resilience initiative explores novel landscape restoration practices given the dynamics and politics of climate change. She is interested in the intersections of political power, environmental activism, and design, particularly as manifest in both public landscapes and the written word.

Guy Nordenson is a structural engineer and Professor at Princeton University. Recent projects include the Kimbell Art Museum in Texas and the National Museum of African American History and Culture in Washington DC. He is co-author, with Catherine Seavitt and Adam Yarinsky, of *On the Water: Palisade Bay* (2010), the foundation of the "Rising Currents" exhibition at the Museum of Modern Art, New York. Nordenson's research initiatives include Structures of Coastal Resilience and the Regional Plan Association's Regional Corridors design competition, both supported by the Rockefeller Foundation.

+ ENGINEERING, ENVIRONMENTAL DESIGN

The failure of New Orleans' levees during Hurricane Katrina in 2005 highlighted a tragic inconsistency in the prevailing perceptions of risk. Ironically, improvements in urban infrastructure, which had lowered the risk associated with frequent but minor flooding, had increased the risk associated with less frequent but major events by making the city's population feel safe enough to expand development to areas that should not have been inhabited. This trend, which geographer Robert W. Kates termed "the safe development paradox," reveals that the management of risk requires difficult choices, particularly the need to balance long- and short-term threats.[1] Yet there is also a balkanization of our efforts to mitigate natural hazards, exacerbated by the fact that all politics are local. For example, in New Orleans (along with the rest of the Gulf Region and the Eastern Seaboard) the flood design standard is typically based on the one-hundred-year storm return period, meaning that structures must be designed to withstand a flood with a 1% chance of occurring in any given year. In the western United States, the 2004 Indian Ocean earthquake and in Japan, the 2011 Tōhoku earthquake, and the tsunamis they caused, have spurred decisions to adhere to the radically longer return period of 2,475 years, commonly used for earthquake hazard mitigation. Adding to the confusion, design guidelines for wind pressures are based on yet other return periods. These wildly varying ranges mean that risk is apportioned unevenly. Worse, residual risk–that of the assumed hazards being greatly exceeded, of climate change, or of levees or other flood control structures unexpectedly failing–is unaccounted for. Given the rapidly evolving dangers of climate change and rising sea levels, the hundred-year flood of yesterday may well be the decadal or even annual event of tomorrow. We are experiencing this shift today.

These inconsistencies in our assessment of risk are problems of science and policy, but also–given the different ways risk is understood and the often unequal ways in which the consequence of residual risks are meted out–of philosophy and social justice. Today, they are problems for art and design as well. As much a cultural construction as a scientific one, risk is all too easily manipulated. Post-9/11, we have been subject both to manufactured fear and to the careless production of residual financial risks. But art and design can mediate between the statistical abstractions of risk and its material and cultural effects; they can also reimagine risk's influence on how we build and inhabit our cities or go about our daily lives. We need an art and design of risk to bring the science of risk back to reality.

Extreme Mapping

After Superstorm Sandy in October 2012, we have witnessed a scramble for new and more-detailed information about the northeast Atlantic coastline, perhaps guided by the fantasy that we could control our environment completely if only we collected as much data as possible. The result is a surge in what was already an upward trend in precision mapping. Various agencies have produced digital elevation models at a 1/9-arc-second resolution (a three-meter grid with a precise spot elevation at each intersection) or gathered high-resolution LiDAR data (provided by airborne laser sweeps of urban landforms producing point clouds with accuracies of within 10 centimeters). Have these digital models finally achieved the infinitesimal detail of Jorge Luis Borges' fabled one-to-one map of the kingdom? FEMA recently issued more-detailed maps of high-risk coastal zones, and New York City has created meticulous post-Sandy risk projections for flood evacuation areas, subdividing its three previous zones into six while also expanding the range of its projections. Simultaneously, in 2015 the New York City Panel on Climate Change (NPCC3) released new climate and sea level rise projections for 2100. All this data, collected from high above the ground, will ostensibly fit right into the abundant adaptation reports and shorefront community handbooks being developed along the East Coast. Amid this precision-mania, we would do well to remember the philosopher and scientist Alfred Korzybski's famous statement: "The map is not the territory."

Left: Subgrade flushing tunnel model at Norton Basin, Rockaway Peninsula, New York (flow lines added).

The most helpful maps may be those that seek not to reproduce a territory's physical terrain but rather engage its culture. One of the most poignant realizations in the tragic aftermath of the 2011 Tōhoku earthquake and tsunami along Japan's northern coast was the wisdom of the tsunami stones–individual stone markers that appear along the coastline of Japan, some almost 600 years old. A typical inscription reads: "High dwellings are the peace and harmony of our descendants. Remember the calamity of the great tsunamis. Do not build any homes below this point." More than an ancient version of FEMA's flood insurance maps or New York City's increasingly detailed evacuation zone maps, these stones mark the high-water point in a way that memorializes past disasters while informing future generations of risk. Like the *horoi* of the ancient Athens agora, the markers are a simple and effective speech act, a way of folding risk into public discourse.[2]

Soft Edges

During the aftermath of the landfall of Sandy, New York City steadfastly refused to abandon its waterfront with the issuance in June 2013 of the *Special Initiative for Rebuilding and Recovery* report generated by Mayor Michael Bloomberg's office. But does this refusal simply justify the former administration's interest in the redevelopment and gentrification of the shoreline territories once occupied by maritime and industrial uses? Throughout the post-Sandy debates in New York and New Jersey, any suggestion of 'retreat'–as the de-population of the waterfront edge has been described–has often been vilified. It appears that, at least within some political jurisdictions, we can only expect more of the kind of wrestling with nature we have long seen in the Sisyphean struggles of the Army Corps of Engineers at the juncture of the Atchafalaya and Mississippi Rivers.

But what does holding the front line versus beating a retreat to high ground really mean? Neither option radically transforms our relationship with water in the urban realm: holding the front line generally means keeping the Anthropocene footprint dry, or elevating it on stilts high above the wet ground. Recent research, including our own, has attempted to muddy and extend this frontline–the shoreline–recognizing it as a dynamic ecological entity.[3] Much of the work in The Museum of Modern Art's 2010 exhibition "Rising Currents: Projects for New York's Waterfront," for example, offered a gradient in lieu of a hard edge. Softer infrastructure might accept water within the urban realm, with waterproof 'flood control' giving way to a wetter 'controlled flooding.' More resilient and adaptable plans for coastal flood protection could provide defense both horizontally–through abating layers of barrier islands, reefs, beaches, dunes, revetments, levees, and gates–and vertically, through the plants, habitats, and ecologies that will give these barriers resilience and malleability. Ultimately, the future of such initiatives lies in local will. Can we develop a strategy of wetness for a city that prefers to be dry?

A recent visit to Venice–that exemplar of amphibious urbanism–reminded us that architectural historian Manfredo Tafuri had deemed it the first modern metropolis because it was the first city to be built without medieval walls. Venice's watery environs actually functioned as military protection: those without knowledge of the lagoon's secret channels and passages, which were easily obscured by the quick removal of the wooden posts that marked their locations, could not safely approach. The city's welfare was dependent on keeping things wet, and so letting the sea in was an act of security. High walls, by contrast, were considered anti-modern; dry land represented nothing but high risk. Imagine something of a 22nd-century Venice for our future coastal cities. Keeping water out may in fact spell destruction, but letting it in could lead to a rich form of adaptive urban survival.

Miasma and Mosquito Trenching

Risk, the landscape, and public health have been inextricably intertwined since the ancient Greeks developed the theory that disease was spread through a noxious miasma in the air, emerging as a poisonous vapor from damp soil. By the 1880s, the new contagionist theory of the germ had gained European support, but dry land was still seen as healthy ground, while wet lands were miserable and unhealthy terrain - dismal swamps, quagmires, bogs. Drainage was the key to health, and gentlemen farmers versed in agricultural engineering, such as George Waring and Frederick Law Olmsted, applied their skills in ceramic tile drainage to urban parks, creating a new field of public sanitation seeking to avoid the spread of cholera, typhoid, and yellow fever. Wetlands disappeared, and 19th-century public spaces such as Central Park were transformed into sanitary mechanical scrubbers, quickly shedding and transporting surface and storm water.

Though better drainage did keep waste water away from drinking water wells, the outbreaks of yellow fever in America, with the extreme example in Memphis in 1878, were not spread by miasma or even inadequate sanitation, but rather a germ vector: the *Aedes* species mosquito, which breeds in stagnant water. Unintentionally, the 19th-century miasmists were successful in stopping the spread of disease, not by preventing the earth's noxious exhalations of bad air but rather by destroying the habitat of the mosquito: stagnant water. The contagionist theory of disease-causing germs, studied simultaneously in the 1870s and 1880s by medical scientists Robert Koch and Louis Pasteur in Europe, quickly replaced that of miasma. After huge losses of United States Army troops to yellow fever in Havana during and after the Spanish-American War of 1898, the army physician Walter Reed successfully proved in August 1900 that the disease was spread by a bite from a germ-infected vector, the *Aedes aegypti* mosquito - now known as the yellow fever mosquito.[4] This is the same mosquito that is the main carrier of today's Zika virus. In

addition to the Zika virus, other mosquito-borne disease risks include the West Nile virus, dengue fever, chikungunya, and several types of encephalitis.

The identification of the mosquito as a disease vector in 1900 led to the massive implementation of extensive wetland 'mosquito trenching,' or the cutting of V-shaped linear open ditches to rapidly drain intertidal marshes. These were first implemented at New York City's intertidal marshes of Jamaica Bay and the southern shore of Staten Island. Like Waring's underground tile drainage of Central Park, marsh trenching created dry ground by whisking away surface water; but these trenches had the unintended consequences of causing serious fragmentation and degradation of the salt marsh complexes, destroying acres of coastal wetland salt marshes. By 1919, the state of New Jersey reported trenching approximately 120,000 acres of salt marsh, which involved the cutting of 18,244,217 linear feet of open ditches (10 inches wide and 24 to 30 inches deep) in order to destroy mosquito-breeding habitats.[5] Indeed, ponded standing water does provide habitat for mosquito larvae, but intertidal action moves water through healthy and robust wetlands that in turn provide the valuable habitat that supports other species that contain mosquito populations.

The recent outbreak of the Zika virus in both North and South America represents another type of risk from climate change and the consequences of migrating disease vectors: public health. Today, international health officials struggling to contain the spread of the Zika virus advise citizens to remove or cover containers or rain gutters that might collect standing water (spraying larvicide over nonresidential areas, which has environmental complications, is not a particularly effective tactic against *Aedes aegyptii*, as this species breeds primarily in gardens and homes). Health risks and unintended environmental consequences must be carefully considered by health officials, landscape architects, and environmental advocates. The development of many new urban green infrastructures, such as bioswales and constructed wetlands, is intent on reducing the negative impacts of the combined sewer systems that discharge wastewater directly into rivers and oceans when overwhelmed by storm water from heavy rains. But the infiltration of potential standing water is the key element of these green infrastructures—current green infrastructural practices advocate absorption and evapotranspiration. The ground need not be bone dry, but it must support the movement of water.

Retrenching Jamaica Bay

Our recent work with the US Army Corps of Engineers at Jamaica Bay, New York, seeks to expand these notions of risk, coastal flooding, environmental vulnerability, and public health. This two-year research investigation and design proposition for a post-Sandy Jamaica Bay, developed by a progressive research laboratory at the City College of New York as part of the Rockefeller Foundation-funded project Structures of Coastal Resilience, posits that the resilient success of the bay's future is dependent upon improving its ecological health.[6] An improved exchange of water and sediment from ocean to bay will lead to both improved water quality and a more robust marsh platform, providing multiple benefits including improved species biodiversity, wave attenuation, wind fetch reduction, coastal erosion protection, and carbon capture. A sound ecological foundation is a critical component of resilient urban climate change adaptation—marshes need to be healthy and robust, not trenched and drained.

Long the dumping ground of New York City, the destination of waste, dead horses, contaminated dredged materials, and even poor and marginalized populations in myriad public housing developments, Jamaica Bay and the Rockaway Peninsula offer the opportunity to recast this embayment as a functioning ecological foreground to the city. And the vast scale of the bay may be embraced as an asset for exploring the development of nature-based features as viable coastal storm risk reduction techniques, as well as engaging a new generation of environmental stewards. Our proposal consists of strategic design recommendations for the Rockaway Peninsula, the central marsh islands, and back-bay communities.

The Jamaica Bay resiliency plan includes three strategies developed through field research and modeling, both physical and digital. The first strategy addresses water quality and the reduction of back-bay flooding via a series of overwash plains, tidal inlets, and flushing tunnels at the Rockaway Peninsula and Floyd Bennett Field. The second strategy develops enhanced verges at Robert Moses' Belt Parkway, elevating coastal edges at vulnerable back-bay communities and managing flood risk with a layered system of marsh terraces, berms, and sunken attenuation forests. The third strategy develops novel techniques of bay nourishment and marsh island restoration through maximizing the efficacy of minimal quantities of dredged material. By harnessing the natural forces of tide and current and constructing elevated linear terraces for sediment trapping at the marsh perimeter with our novel technique named the "atoll terrace/island motor," the marsh islands are enabled to migrate upward with sea level rise. A resilient marsh ecosystem provides coastal storm risk management services to adjacent communities through wind and wave attenuation, delivering maximum immediate benefits for both vulnerable communities and the disappearing salt marsh islands. Here, risk reduction is not achieved through drainage, but through intertidal flooding and its sediment delivery—a new *aqueous* urbanism.

1 R.W. Kates, C. E. Colten, S. Laska & S. P. Leatherman, "Reconstruction of New Orleans After Hurricane Katrina: A Research Perspective," *Proceedings of the National Academy of Sciences* 103, no. 40 (2006): 14653–60.

2 Josiah Ober, "Greek Horoi: Artifactual Texts and the Contingency of Meaning," in David B. Small (ed.), *Methods in the Mediterranean: Historical and Archaeological Views on Texts and Archaeology* (Leiden, The Netherlands: E. J. Brill, 1995), 91–123.

3 Guy Nordenson, Catherine Seavitt & Adam Yarinsky, *On the Water: Palisade Bay* (Stuttgart, Germany: Hatje Cantz Verlag, 2010).

4 For the history of this discovery, see Howard A. Kelly, *Walter Reed and Yellow Fever* (Baltimore, Maryland: The Medical Standards Book Company Publishers, 1906). For an analysis of the ethics of Reed's medical experimentation on human subjects, see Susan E. Lederer, *Subjected to Science: Human Experimentation in America before the Second World War* (Baltimore, Maryland: Johns Hopkins University Press, 1997).

5 Thomas J. Headlee, "The Mosquitoes of New Jersey and their Control," in *New Jersey Agricultural Experiment Stations Bulletin* 348 (New Brunswick, New Jersey, 1921).

6 See complete documentation of all four research sites of Structures of Coastal Resilience, including Jamaica Bay, New York; Narragansett Bay, Rhode Island; Atlantic City, New Jersey; and Norfolk, Virginia at www.structuresofcoastalresilience.org.

AMERICA'S PETROCHEMICAL GARDEN

BILLY FLEMING

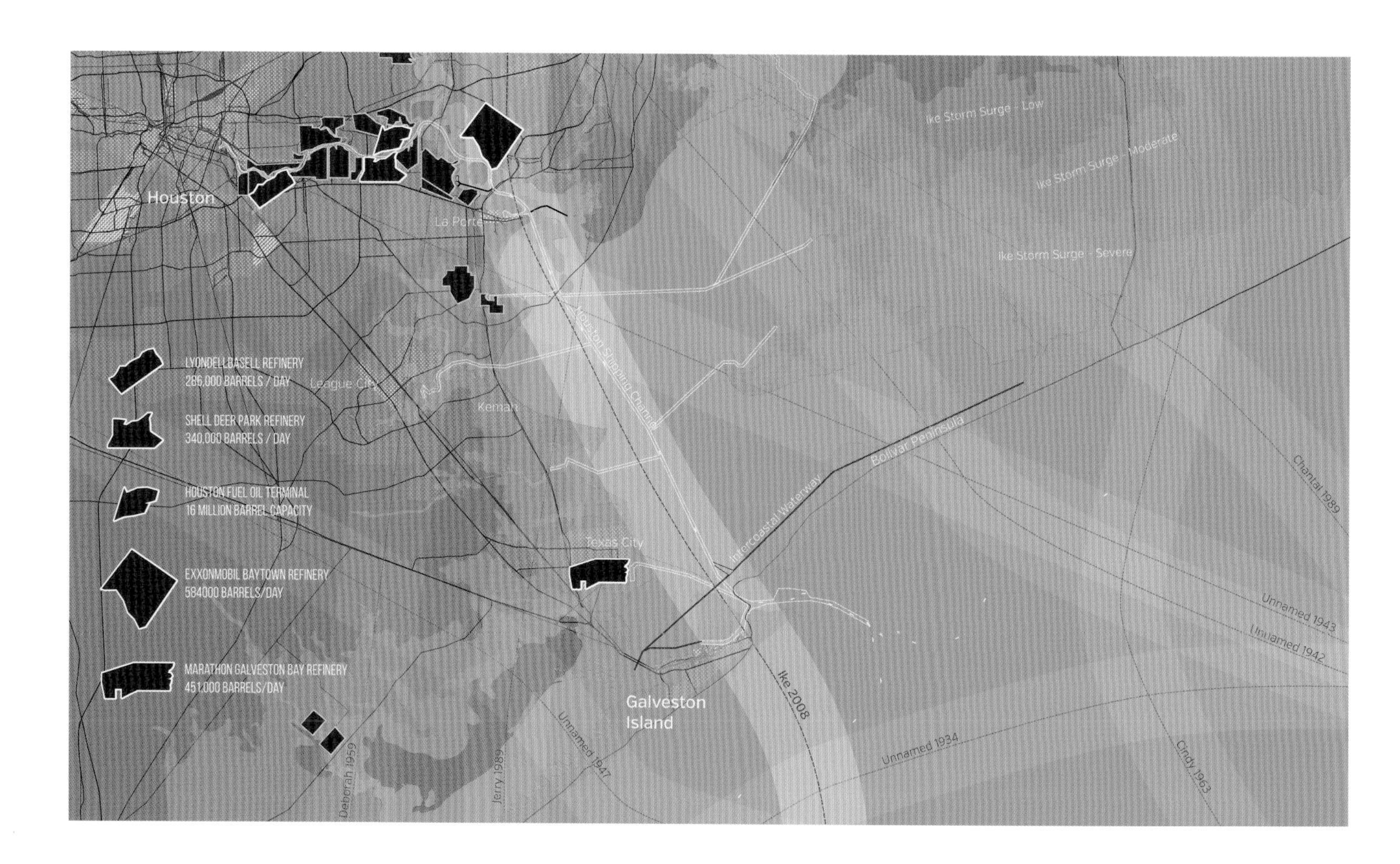

Billy Fleming is Research Coordinator for the Ian McHarg Center in the University of Pennsylvania's School of Design, where he earned a PhD in City and Regional Planning. His research is focused on the pathways to implementation for and performative value of coastal green infrastructure in vulnerable communities. Prior to joining Penn, Fleming worked in the White House Domestic Policy Council during President Barack Obama's first term.

+ PLANNING, RESILIENCE THEORY

Previous: The Bolivar Peninsula following Hurricane Ike.

Above: The Galveston Bay region, highlighting petrochemical facilities and previous hurricane paths.

On September 14, 2008, the Galveston Bay region lay in ruins.[1] Three-quarters of the island's homes, businesses, and other structures lay scattered across the salty brine remnants of Hurricane Ike.[2] The low, undulating dune system that once rimmed the seaward edge of the Texas coast was now imperceptible. A clear path of erasure stretched from the beaches of Galveston Island to the Houston suburbs of Kemah and Baytown. Fish flopped and snakes—hordes of them—slithered across FM3005, the westward evacuation route washed out long before Ike made landfall.[3] By the time the insurance agents and actuaries finished surveying the aftermath, Ike's damage toll rose to almost 150 billion dollars. Mostly absent from the discourse on landscape architecture and resilience, Hurricane Ike stands as the second-most destructive storm in US history.[4]

That's because on September 15, 2008, Lehman Brothers filed for Chapter 11 bankruptcy protection and became the opening salvo of the global financial meltdown known as the Great Recession. As a result, the national press and the federal government quickly pivoted away from the work of disaster recovery in Galveston Bay and towards staving off a national economic collapse. This left the region's residents without the attention or the resources that typically flow in the aftermath of a storm. Nearly a decade later, the region has largely recovered from the worst of Ike, but over the course of that decade, little has been done to deal with the surge and sea level rise related risks facing the region. The region remains one of the nation's most vulnerable territories.

The Galveston Bay Region

Galveston Bay and its distributaries—the San Jacinto, Buffalo Bayou, and Trinity Rivers—represent the largest ecological system within the nation's fourth-largest and fastest-growing urban region, the Houston metropolitan area.[5] More than six million people reside in and around the Houston-Galveston region. Half of those residents occupy a marshy surge zone encircling the Bay. There, a sprawling patchwork of tract homes and wide, winding roadways blanket the low-lying, flood-prone landscape of Houston. Though the presence of these homes in the surge zone is a problem unto itself, their vulnerability is complicated by the lax land development regulations in Houston and its suburbs. These homes were developed in a flood-prone environment according to building codes that do not consider flood-proofing or free-boarding in their stipulations. Seasonal flooding already imperils these homes and residents each spring. The surge from the Gulf of Mexico is coming for them too.[6]

The rationale behind building cheap homes in a flood-prone landscape is clear. The suburban communities encircling Houston were simply vying for their share of the region's booming population. Spurred on by the growth in oil and petrochemical industries over the last two decades, Texas City, Kemah, League City, Baytown, and others each hoped to capture a larger portion of the property tax receipts these new residents would provide. In Texas, where property taxes are very high in order to offset the absence of a statewide income tax, this led suburban communities to compete in a race to the bottom for new residents.[7] Nowhere was this process more evident than in the surge zone surrounding Houston. There, cheap land and cheap housing coalesced to pack hundreds of thousands of new people into a high-risk landscape.

Houston's suburbs came to embody much of what Joel Kotkin refers to as "opportunity urbanism," or the notion that a deregulated land development market is the key to creating an affordable, virtuous metropolis.[8] But the low cost of the region's housing market came at a steep price: ecologically and socially destructive sprawl. Kotkin's obsession with cheap housing belies the preciousness of inducing low- and middle-income families into flood-prone, poorly-built homes. If there is no such thing as a free lunch, neither is there such thing as a cheap home - the costs are just borne in other ways, at other times.

The magnet that has drawn—and continues to draw—so many people to the Houston region is the booming petrochemical industry headquartered in and around Galveston Bay. Multi-billion dollar investments in oil refining capacity, petrochemical processing and storage, and port infrastructure constantly push the region's center of economic gravity towards the water's edge. As a result, Galveston Bay is emblematic of the risks posed by climate change to most port cities: the social and economic fortunes of the region are dependent upon proximity and access to open water.

The region already boasts the largest cluster of petrochemical activity in the nation, with nearly 30% of all domestic refining capacity operating in and around the Bay.[9] It is the petrochemical capital of the United States, if not the world. It's also home to the nation's second (Houston), fourth (Beaumont), thirteenth (Texas City), eighteenth (Port Arthur), and forty-ninth (Galveston) largest ports by tonnage in the US.[10] All of these port facilities are expected to grow as a result of the Panama Canal expansion.[11] Many of them also abut, intersect, or otherwise conflict with the sprawling patchwork of suburban homes that characterize the region.

Put differently, the fastest growing metropolitan region in the US is rapidly surrounding the nation's densest cluster of petrochemical facilities. Placing residential homes alongside heavy industry poses its own set of unique problems. All of those risks are complicated and exacerbated by rising seas. As a result, the residents of Galveston Bay face more than the risk of flooding. They face the risk of exposure to the petrochemical slurry being stored and refined alongside their neighborhoods. They face the risk of being left with a toxic, uninhabitable community in the aftermath of the next storm.

Hurricane Ike

These risks were exposed in dramatic fashion by Hurricane Ike. Though the storm came ashore 30 miles west of Galveston Bay, surge levels in and around the region reached 18 feet. That was high enough to overtop many of the community's seawalls and levees. It was also enough to leave a quarter-million Texans homeless and to inflict nearly 40 billion dollars in property damage.[12]

Though Ike's briny flotsam was quickly removed, the region's endemic flood risk was not so easily disposed. Many of the homes, critical facilities, and infrastructural networks damaged by the storm were simply rebuilt to their pre-storm specifications (with the new water treatment plant along the North Bay a notable exception). Were a future storm to strike at a slightly different angle or with slightly greater wind speed or surface area, engineers and marine scientists at Texas A&M University, Jackson State University, and the US Army Corps of Engineers predict that as many as 60% of the region's petrochemical facilities would experience a critical failure known as a natech: natural hazard triggering technological disasters. Nearly two-thirds of the petrochemicals stored and processed in Galveston Bay—over three billion barrels of oil—are at risk of being spilled across its landscape.[13]

The scale of such a spill is difficult to fathom. To put it into context, know this: the BP Deepwater Horizon Spill poured five million barrels into the Gulf of Mexico. That was enough to alter the ecology of the entire area, devastating shrimp and shellfish populations and causing a toxic bioaccumulation of oil in fisheries throughout the Gulf. It also decimated coastal vegetation and triggered the rapid denudation of dune systems, beaches, and wildlife habitat along the coast. Nearly seven years after the spill, the marine ecosystem of the region appears inexorably changed.

In Galveston, such a spill would place more oil into a smaller geographic area; the toxic slurry of oil and gas would be less diluted than that of the BP Deepwater Horizon spill. Worse,

1

2

3

1. The Great Storm of 1900 flattened more than 80% of Galveston's structures and remains the deadliest natural disaster in US history.
2. The rebuild following the 1900 storm included raising the topographic profile of Galveston by more than 12 feet in some locations.
3. An important defense against future storm surges is the Galveston Seawall, a 10-mile-long, 17-foot tall surge barrier.

it would place people's lives and livelihoods at greater risk of exposure, and it would require a more difficult and expensive clean-up operation than that required for an offshore drilling rig. A direct hit from a large hurricane to the petrochemical complex of Galveston Bay is perhaps the greatest and most-imminent threat to the public health, safety, and welfare of the United States. And the risk will only grow as more people pour into the region, more petrochemicals move through it, and sea levels continue to rise.

Disastrous Legacies

Before speculating on the potential futures for Galveston Bay, it is important to examine the legacy of disaster and redevelopment in the region. One event, in particular, irrevocably altered the region: the Great Storm of 1900. The deadliest storm in US history, it killed more than 8,000 people and razed most of the region's structures.[14]

Prior to 1900, Galveston was home to the second-busiest port by volume on the Gulf Coast. It competed with the ports of New Orleans and Chicago for the booming commodities market flowing through Middle America. After the storm, the shipping industry migrated northward en masse, abandoning the highly exposed landscape of the barrier island in favor of the protected harbors of West Bay. Without a strong port to lure back the island's population, Texas officials considered abandoning Galveston altogether; but the Army considered it too important to the economic and national security of the nation. As a result, they invested heavily in the island's reconstruction, building what would become one of the 20th century's greatest feats of engineering: a 17-foot, island-wide seawall backfilled to raise the grade of the island by as much as 12 feet.

Other US cities—Chicago, for instance—embarked on large-scale grade-raising projects around this time too. But those efforts typically focused on adding three-to-five feet of elevation across small portions of a city. None approach the scale or scope of Galveston.[15] Every road, structure, fire hydrant, rail track, and infrastructural network had to be hydraulically lifted, backfilled, and reintegrated into the island's new topography. To complete the project, a fleet of international dredge ships was diverted from the African coast to Galveston Bay.

Those ships were met by tens of thousands of laborers who, in 1904, began the process of reshaping Galveston Island. Entire neighborhoods were lifted, flooded, and backfilled with dredge material over the course of a decade. By 1915, the grade-raising and the first segment of the seawall were finally complete. Where sand dunes and salt cedars once stood, Galveston had erected a coastal fortress that stood in stark relief to the sprawling, featureless plain of Southeast Texas. In the century since its construction, no storm has ever breached the island's seawall. The project's success as an instrument of flood-protection became a driving force behind the region's widespread support for technological, resistance-based approaches to risk reduction.

Coastal Resilience in Galveston Bay

Driven by the performative success of the seawall, a coalition of policy, scientific, and design experts have begun exploring a variety of approaches to resilience-building in Galveston Bay. Their efforts have yielded three distinct project proposals: the Ike Dike, the Centennial Gate System, and the Ring Levee System.

The Ike Dike is based on the concept of a coastal spine. It is a 50-mile-long network of structurally reinforced dunes, towering seawalls, and floodgates aimed at resisting the wave and surge energy produced by tropical storms. Promulgated by Bill Merrell, the project represents a wholesale adoption of the resistance philosophy common to engineering theories of resilience.[16] The Ike Dike is essentially a massive fortification project, one that stretches across the most densely-settled portions of the Galveston Bay region. Its cost estimates range from three-to-eight billion dollars, though no one has yet determined how extensive its foundation will need to be.[17]

The conceptual parallels between the Ike Dike and the Dutch methods of flood risk reduction are obvious and openly acknowledged by Merrell and other proponents of the project. In Holland's coastal defense system, structural protections—be they walls, levees, or hybridized dune-wall systems like the Ike Dike—are deployed to keep water out of its major cities. Though the Dutch methods have kept Amsterdam and Rotterdam dry for more than a half-century, their approach has also led to creation of one of the world's largest hypoxic zones. In Galveston, where the region depends upon a vibrant marine ecosystem to sustain its local economy, the tradeoff between a half-century of protection and ecological devastation is harder to justify. A massive coastal barrier would irrevocably alter the Bay's ecology by altering sediment flows to and through the Bay, and by reducing its tidal prism, or the exchange of fresh and saltwater unique to estuarine environments.[18] The Dutch are now working to ameliorate the damage wrought by their resistance-based approach to coastal resilience. Ike Dike advocates will need to prove that importing ideas from Holland to Texas will not force them to do the same.

Formulated in response to the ecologically destructive potential of the Ike Dike, the Centennial Gate System adopts a radically different approach to flood risk reduction. Rather than armoring the coastline, it calls for a single, structural intervention at the mouth of the Houston Ship Channel: a retractable flood barrier. Elsewhere, the system relies on so called nature-based strategies to reduce surge impacts. Using the results of SLOSH[19] modeling exercises, it places oyster reefs, wetland restorations, and dune complexes in strategic positions throughout the Bay. However, its cost has yet to be estimated.

Devised by researchers at Rice University, the Centennial Gate System treats much of Galveston Island as a sacrificial zone. Drawing from ecological resilience theory, it uses the island as a buffer or shock absorber for the rest of the region.[20] Historically,

IKE DIKE

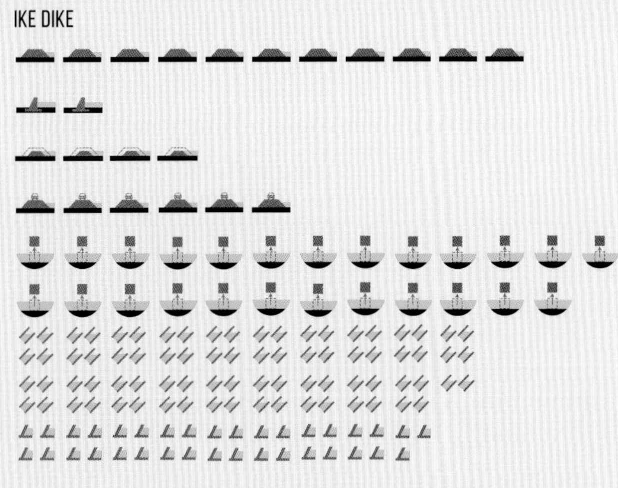

CENTENNIAL GATE SYSTEM

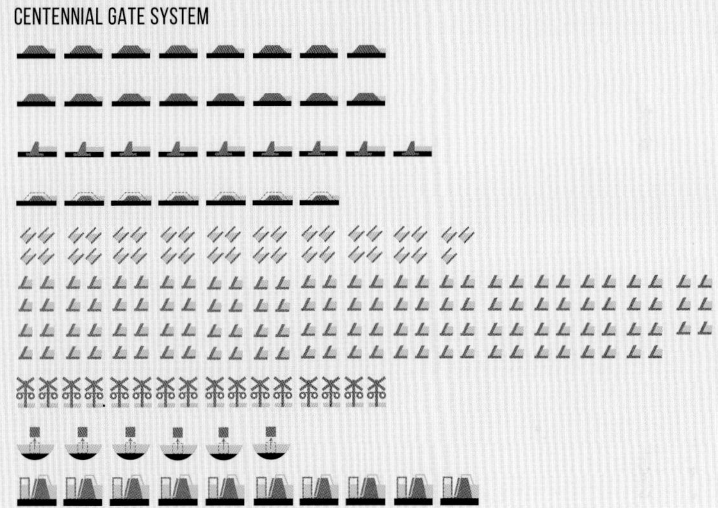

RING LEVEE SYSTEM

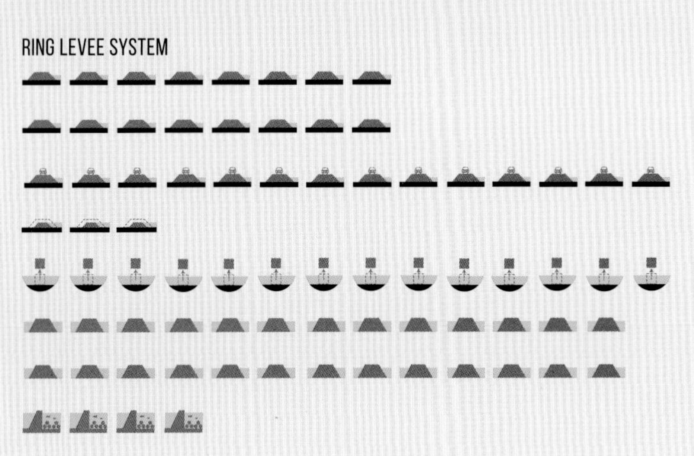

10,000 ft
New Levee

10,000 ft
T Wall

10,000 ft
Levee Addn

10,000 ft
Road Levee

1
Sea Gate

4 Drainage
Structures

4 Road
Gates

1 Railroad
Gate

1 Pump
Station

1M CY
Dredge Levee

1 M CY
Oyster
Reefs

1 "Major storms make landfall in the region once every eleven years" Federal Emergency Management Agency, "Disaster Declarations by Year," https://www.fema.gov/disasters/grid/year.

2 Texas Engineering Extension Service (TEES), "Hurricane Ike Impact Report" (2012), http://thestormresource.com/Resources/Documents/Full_Hurricane_Ike_Impact_Report.pdf.

3 Interview with local elected official, Galveston, TX (March 21, 2016).

4 TEES, "Hurricane Ike Impact Report."

5 Houston-Galveston Area Council, "Regional Economic Development Plan," http://www.h-gac.com/community/gcedd/regional-economic-development-plan.aspx.

6 John Lomax, "Is Houston Sustainable? A Flood Postmortem," *Texas Monthly* (April 25 2016).

7 Jaime Masterson, et al., *Planning for Community Resilience: A Handbook for Reducing Vulnerability to Disasters* (Washington, DC: Island Press, 2014).

8 Joel Kotkin, *Opportunity Urbanism: Creating Cities for Upward Mobility* (Houston, TX: Center for Opportunity Urbanism, 2014).

9 Greater Houston Partnership, "Houston's Economy," http://www.houston.org/economy/index.html#Energy.

10 Bureau of Transportation Statistics, "Tonnage of Top 50 US Water Ports, Ranked by Total Tons," http://www.rita.dot.gov/bts/sites/rita.dot.gov.bts/files/publications/national_transportation_statistics/html/table_01_57.html.

11 Brian Davis, Rob Holmes & Brett Milligan, "Isthmus: Panama Canal Expansion," *Places Journal* (2015) https://placesjournal.org/article/isthmus-panama-canal-expansion.

12 TEES, "Hurricane Ike Impact Report."

13 Nicholas Santella, Laura Steinberg & Gloria Aguirra, "Empirical Estimation of the Conditional Probability of Natech Events within the United States," *Risk Analysis* 31, no. 6 (2011): 951–68.

14 William Merrell, *Henry Sampson and the Great Galveston Storm* (Sarasota: First Edition Design Publishing, 2015).

this has been the role of barrier islands – to buffer the mainland from the worst effects of tropical storms. Of course, this precedent predates human settlement and its application is questionable in Galveston. Nevertheless, it departs from the resistance logic of the Ike Dike by restoring and creating new ecological features to create a redundant and less intense system of flood protection. But many of the plan's skeptics worry that its nature-based strategies are treated as ancillary components of the system and that they might be dropped in the event of cost overruns. One went so far as to remark that it is "window dressing meant to woo the environmental community. We'll never do any restoration work in the middle of the bay. The shipping industry would never allow it!"[21]

Drawing on the popularity of Galveston Island's century-old seawall, the proposed Ring Levee system seeks to employ a resistance approach to surge protection in the region.[22] Unlike the Ike Dike, however, it does not aim to protect the entire coast. Rather, the Ring Levee system proposes to encircle the densest clusters of population with levees and to treat the remaining landscape as sacrificial. It is a low-cost alternative to the Ike Dike and Centennial Gate system, relying on neither a complex floodgate operation nor the inclusion of nature-based strategies in its scheme. Instead, the Ring Levee system would simply raise and harden the edge, transforming the area from a fluid coastal zone to a static coastline. It is an implicit endorsement of the notion that nature and humanity cannot coexist, that they must be harshly delineated.

If built, the Ring Levee system would be vulnerable to two sources of failure. One is that the management of flood protection infrastructure is highly decentralized in the US. The federal government builds coastal infrastructure projects and local governments maintain them. The problem with this model of governance is that few, if any, local governments possess the financial or technical capacity necessary to take on that maintenance. It is what undermined the levees in New Orleans long before Katrina. It would likely undermine the Ring Levees in Galveston too. The second source of potential failure is a result of the method used by the Army Corps for evaluating projects. Under this system, the Corps is forced to make the economic benefits of a project its primary concern – commercial activity, industrial facilities, and property values protected. The environmental impacts of a project are only considered qualitatively and, often, as an ancillary consideration. Ecosystem services cannot be considered by the Corps.

All that matters under this system is the maximization of the costs-benefit ratio. This means that the levee heights would not be determined by the amount of flood protection the community desires, but by the point at which the marginal benefit of additional height begins to decline. The result would be a cheaper project that provides less overall protection to the Galveston Bay region. This is not the fault of the Corps. Their operations are governed by congressional mandate and their method of project evaluation cannot change without an act of Congress. This does not bode well for the security of the region.[23]

Unnatural Futures

Implicit in the proposals for coastal resilience in Galveston is the idea that nature and culture can be decoupled. Only the Centennial Gate system considers nature-based strategies as a potential form of protection, but even it relegates those elements to an ancillary position. All three proposals call for a degree of resistance-driven resilience drawn from engineering. That approach is particularly salient in Galveston, where flood-risk is a part of everyday life and where a century of evidence shows that such an approach can be effective. From the perspective of many in the region, nature simply cannot be trusted to perform the serious work of engineers.

Their perspective has an audience beyond Galveston. Despite the doubts cast on the resistance approach to resilience by Hurricanes Katrina and Sandy in New Orleans and New York, grey infrastructure continues to proliferate along the coast. Green infrastructure has thus far been relegated to renderings – the preferred choice of an imagined world, not the real one. But building walls means building an ecology. It means altering ecosystems and hydrology, as well as housing markets and supply chains. Projects like the seawall in Galveston and the floodwalls in New Orleans create winners and losers. Some gain land, property value, and ecosystem services at the expense of others. The net benefit calculation used by the Corps to select which project is built does not consider the distribution of its spoils.

In Galveston, there are unique risks to consider. Not only are hundreds of thousands of residents living in poorly-built homes within the surge zone, but they are doing so beside the largest cluster of petrochemical facilities in the nation. The death and destruction that accompanies all coastal storms would be amplified by the very real possibility that this vulnerable landscape could be transformed into a toxic one. Unlike the BP Deepwater Horizon Spill, a petrochemical disaster in Galveston Bay would not be miles offshore and diluted by the whole of the Gulf of Mexico. It would be in homes and streets, rivers and farms, schools and businesses. It would preclude most residents from returning home, and it would force those that did to live in a toxic, cancerous landscape of oil, chemicals, and industrial waste.

Nature-based strategies cannot erase this risk, but they can and should be a part of minimizing it. Dune systems can deflect surge energy, reducing the risk of a catastrophic hit to the petrochemical cluster in Galveston. Wetlands and marshes can help to filter and retain toxins that inevitably spill during a disaster. Oyster and shellfish reefs–though unable to contribute to the reduction of surge risk[24]–could help filter the remaining toxins from the bay. Toxins would surely remain, but in proportions small enough to be flushed from the system over time by the dynamic processes of the bay. Relying solely upon walls, levees, and structural protections to keep the water out is the best way to ensure that an ecological approach to risk reduction proves unattainable in Galveston. The same protections built to keep the water out would inevitably hold the floodwaters and petrochemicals in when breached. Yet, the Army Corps' method of project evaluation precludes them from considering nature-based strategies as viable options in the densely settled areas of Galveston Bay. This is a product of our perception that nature is capricious – a construct that landscape architects have historically harnessed. Framing what amounts to green infrastructure as a nature-based approach to coastal resilience immediately casts all other approaches as more serious works of engineering. It also casts a veil of permanence over structural, resistance-based resilience. The reality of coastal resilience planning is that no intervention–whether a Dutch Works-style floodgate or Living Breakwaters-style oyster reef–can be considered a solution to the problem of sea level rise. There are no solutions, only interventions that forestall and minimize the inevitable loss of land, livelihood, and ecosystem function that are coming.

The challenge to coastal planners, then, is less about how to solve a problem and more about how to manage it over time, using an array of approaches that are soft and hard, nature-based and resistance-oriented. Nature-based strategies have advantages: they are cheap to build and maintain, they allow for habitats to migrate and novel ecosystems to form, they provide human health benefits and other ecosystem services and, most importantly, they give communities time to cope with and plan for the coming erasure. Nature-based strategies can allow cities to think more purposefully, outside the frame of crisis-driven urbanization, about what to protect and what to surrender to the sea.

15 William Cronon, *Nature's Metropolis: Chicago and the Great West* (New York: W.W. Norton & Company, 1991).

16 Billy Fleming, "Lost in Translation: The Authorship Structure and Argumentation of Resilience Theory," *Landscape Journal* 35, no. 1 (2016): 13–26.

17 Center for Texas Beaches and Shores, "The Economic Impact of the Ike Dike," http://www.tamug.edu/ikedike/images_and_documents/Economic_Impact_Report.pdf.

18 Interview with local marine scientist, Galveston, TX (March 24, 2016).

19 The Sea, Lake, and Overland Surge from Hurricanes (SLOSH) model is a GIS-based simulation program used by the Federal Emergency Management Agency, the USACE, and academic marine scientists to estimate storm-related damages in coastal communities. See, http://www.nhc.noaa.gov/surge/slosh.php.

20 Fleming, "Lost in Translation."

21 Interview with public official, Galveston, TX (March 29, 2016).

22 Fleming, "Lost in Translation."

23 The Gulf Coast Community Protection and Recovery District, "Phase 2 Report: Surge Suppression Alternatives," http://www.gccprd.com/pdfs/01%20-%20FINAL%20GCCPRD_Phase%202%20Report_022416.pdf.

24 Committee on US Army Corps of Engineers Water Resources Science, Engineering, and Planning: Coastal Risk Reduction. *Reducing Coastal Risk on the East and Gulf Coasts* (Washington, DC: National Academies Press, 2014).

IN CONVERSATION WITH

STEPHEN KIERAN + JAMES TIMBERLAKE

With the recent release of *Alluvium*, Philadelphia-based architects **Stephen Kieran** and **James Timberlake** collate the results of their seven-year design-research inquiry into Dhaka, Bangladesh. One of the most densely populated cities on Earth, prone to devastating floods, and facing the very real risks of earthquakes and sea level rise, Dhaka has some of the world's most extreme urban conditions. Landscape architect Joshua Seyfried interviewed the authors on behalf of LA+.

+ Dhaka is facing incredible challenges, a booming population, widespread vulnerability to sea level rise, and a lack of institutional capacity for managing these problems. What makes you think Dhaka will succeed where other cities in the developing world have failed?

SK Because of how far behind they are in the development string compared to other developing nations, there may be some opportunities in Dhaka that don't exist elsewhere in terms of how they can start to address some of these pressing problems – especially since they don't have infrastructure in place yet, and on many levels haven't begun. It's kind of like the cell phone argument, those nations that didn't invest in all the wire and infrastructure are in some ways better off than those that came earlier. If you start to think about it in that way, they still have room to make decisions in terms of how infrastructure is managed. Take power for example, there are already entities doing a lot for rural Bangladesh by pushing solar power. They're not putting in transmission infrastructure, they're decentralizing and using solar. You can start to expand that idea across the board and come up with some different development models for other parts of the developing world.

JT I agree with much of what Steve said but I want to contextualize it a little differently. They do have water and infrastructure, they do have traffic problems; what they don't have are proper sewage and water supply chains, all of which require basically digging the city up or just setting the old city totally aside yet again – which they have already done twice before. Secondly, they've made some bad choices and because they are an emerging [alleged] democracy they're more interested in politics at the moment than solutions. Thirdly, at this particular point, Dhaka is completely beholden to money coming from external sources, and as we all know if you are not in control of that you can't control the outcome.

The infrastructure projects that they are currently working on are primarily foreign led, so they are only as good as the energy that is coming from those particular sources. That said, there are countries other than the United States that are investing in them heavily and there are infrastructure projects being completed. Those projects, though, are ignoring the problem they have at hand: they're doing fly-overs instead of trying to address traffic problems at the street level. The second positive is that Bangladesh has an incredibly intelligent, well-educated populous with an immense amount of energy and they want to improve. There is now even a wealthy populace that wants to reinvest in the country. Lastly, the net positive goes back to Steve's comment, they are arriving late to these problems, they can skip over tried tactics that haven't worked in other places and try to invest in those things that do work. There is serendipity to the positives.

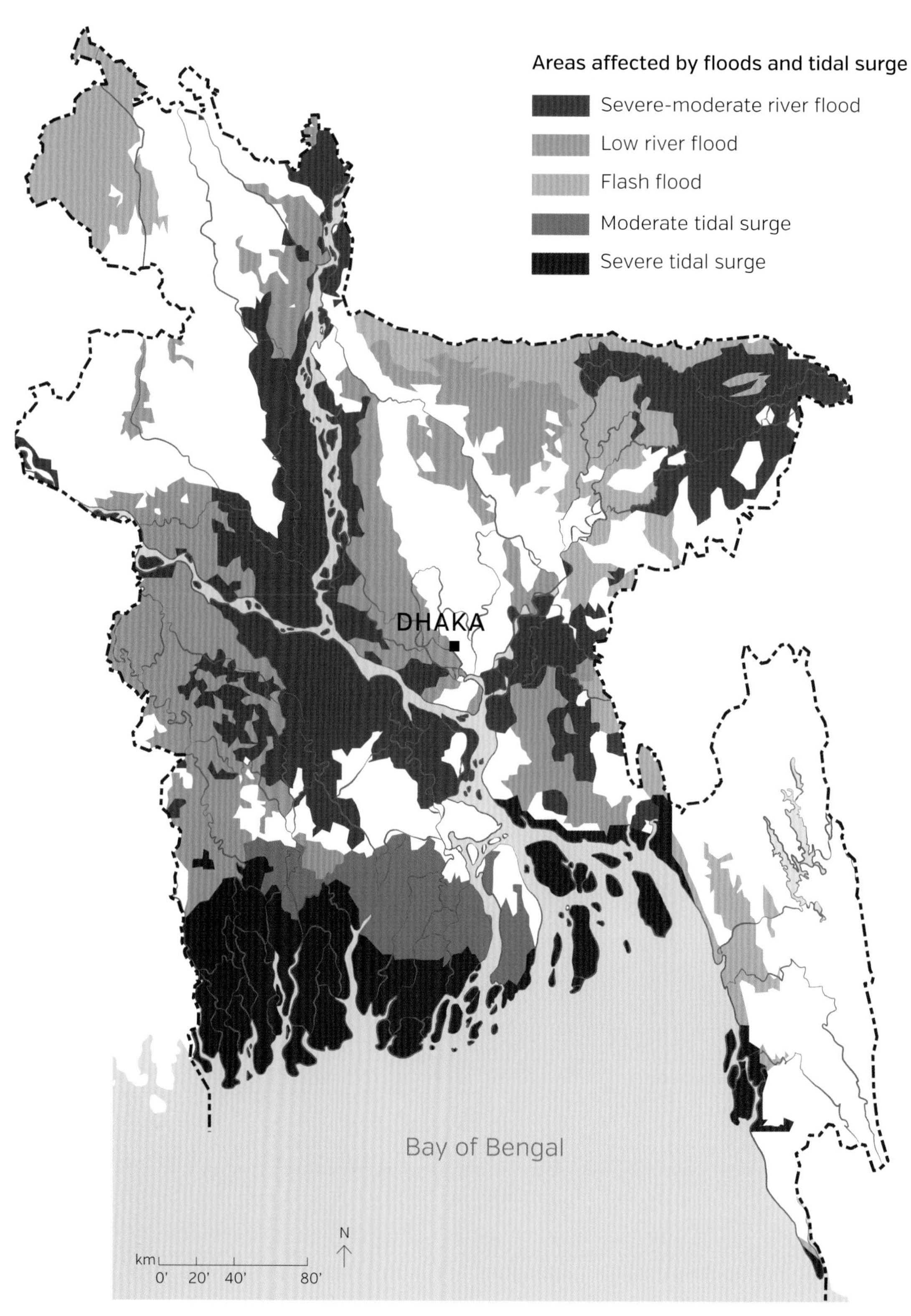

Above: Massive rainfall, runoff from the Himalayas and the entire Ganges-Brahmaputra river basin, and cyclone-driven tidal surges combine with the extremely low geographic elevation to put 80% of Bangladesh at risk of flooding.

+ Bangladesh is often discussed within the context of housing and population growth but sea level rise is going to have a much broader impact across the region. How do you see the forces of climate change, population growth, and industrialization overlapping?

JT I am a firm believer that we are not just going to stand by and let sea level rise continue without addressing both the symptoms and the potential outcomes. Are they going to lose the mangroves? Probably; they will not act in time. Are they going to end up with sea level potentially at Dhaka's doorstep? I doubt it. I think interventions will happen in the interim; those will also likely have impacts on industrialization. Bangladesh is a leader in cheap labor-sourcing, but my suspicion is that there is already intent to get that under control and as they do so, as wages rise and other things happen, it's going to slow the avalanche of industrialization in Bangladesh. Unlike Vietnam and China, there is a limited capacity: they do not have much land mass. The population growth and the industrialization and the agriculture and the sea level rise are competing for the same land. This is going to mean hard decisions from the government. The folks there are already voting with their feet; they are already moving to Dubai, Africa, and India.

SK The potential problem is so extreme that it is hard to imagine it can happen. The consequences will be overwhelming and have ramifications across not just the region but the world. Given the statistical profile of the place, it's for good cause that the UN has declared it the most threatened place on Earth in terms of sea level rise. About 10% (15 million) of the population live along the Bay of Bengal, and it seems increasingly inevitable that there is going to be enough flooding in the near future to completely displace that population. The nation itself has high ground only on the eastern and northern edges. Dhaka is roughly 10 meters (30 feet) above sea level and you can already start to imagine a population half the size of the United States condensed into a state that is roughly the size of Iowa, that is now having to condense further. The population management consequences are pretty extreme. The stem of migration from rural to urban in Dhaka is going to be difficult to manage with sea level rise; how they don't overwhelm Dhaka seems to me the most central question. Can they decentralize some of their future growth and start to develop other urban centers besides Dhaka? Those are national decisions: there is going to have to be policy making. Do they have the will and the ability to do it? They are resourceful: historically they've demonstrated the ability to live with water in ways that are catastrophic to us but are managed daily life for them. Will they continue to be that resourceful in this water-to-land relationship in the future? I'm more optimistic about their capacity on some levels than I am ours!

JT I disagree. I think you're speaking about 50% of the population – the 50% of the population that is undereducated and vulnerable and does not have the capacity to even go on weather.com and get the hell out of the way. The biggest problem is that their leadership is so paralyzed by their own political gain rather than serving the people. So the 50% that is underserved are going to continue to be underserved.

+ There is minimal land within the country suitable for construction and the bulk of what we do see is the result of dredging and filling with river sand. Do you see this continuing to reshape the waterfront around Dhaka?

SK Yes. The extent of the sand filling around Dhaka now is like a cancer. If you look at it, there are patches of water in-between but they are filling in year by year. What is going to stem the pattern?

JT It's a cancer...or a prophylactic. The reason we don't like it is because it is land grabbing and illegal. The moment it becomes government subsidized and legal because they need the land in order to create the space, that shifts the conversation to something totally different. I would argue that the sand filling and dredging is going to become legalized.

SK Legalization would suggest that there could be planning associated with it. Some of what we explored with our work with students over the years is how to equalize the water with the land and do it in a planned way instead of just filling in everything. If it is legalized (and I tend to agree that it has to be over time), then eventually if so much of it is happening then governments have limited choices. They can choose to keep turning their backs to it and not deal with it or they can legalize it and manage it.

+ Let's change pace and take a look at your experiences in the slums of Dhaka. One of the things that *Alluvium* is most successful at is arguing that the slums are not going to disappear so we might as well maximize their potential.

SK Certainly, we could see a lot of development in the slums over the several years that we went into Dhaka. Initially, they were all single-story dwellings but on our last trip we were starting to see two-story dwellings. During some of the earlier trips we saw relatively little infrastructure and since they are all illegal developments that the government does not recognize, you have a question of how you are going to install infrastructure in something that theoretically doesn't exist. Despite this, we started to see infrastructural transformations within the slums. Apart from the additional stories, we saw schools run by NGOs that weren't there when we first started visiting. We started to see community gardens and open space and informal leadership systems that have developed over the years in the absence of government.

JT Let me answer this as a sociologist and anthropologist. There are three drivers: first is the family unit, second is economics, and third is transport or mobility. If you think about the 1930s in the United States, families were geographically isolated by their inability to get around. Those that had access to a car, like my grandparents from southern Ohio, could pick up their family and move to Pittsburgh and try to find work. They can't do that so much in Bangladesh. They can get on a bus that gets them to Dhaka but there is really nowhere else. Secondly, because of the industrialization in Bangladesh, jobs are principally in and around Dhaka. Until those become decentralized to other cities in Bangladesh in order to take the pressure off Dhaka, not much will change. For example, transporting clothing produced in the far reaches of Bangladesh back into Dhaka is a huge problem. There is a major gap in infrastructure from the point of production to the point of distribution. Until they improve this, economies will remain centralized.

+ Speaking of permanence and development, there is a recent article in *National Geographic* revealing the discovery of a mega-thrust fault which Dhaka sits on. One of the researchers quoted in the article describes the city as having been built on "a bowl of Jell-O." What does this mean for the vulnerability of future and current settlements?

SK Clearly one of the most-dangerous materials to build on is sand, and the so-called turtle-back of Dhaka is clay, but everything they are doing to expand the city outward is being built on sand.

JT I think this is more akin to Loma Prieta, 1989, in San Francisco. The alluvium of San Francisco is a microcosm of the alluvium of Dhaka. I believe that there is some equation there and that when they get the right size quake in the right location this thing is going to move the Jell-O around in such a way that is going to take the city down. Unfortunately, you are going to see a magnitude of collapses not unlike the 2013 Rana Plaza garment factory collapse, and that came down on its own without a shake.

SK One of the real fears is for the concrete construction. In some ways the lower-rise informal dwellings may fare better because they are loose-frame buildings that can move, but there is plenty of reason to assume the concrete work is not up to contemporary standards for earthquake resistance and that is the fearsome part.

JT But on a bandwidth of disasters, let's talk about where they think this one is. It is likely off the register!

SK They are not even talking about the 18th-century earthquake that moved the river over 100 miles. At the time there were not nearly as many people living in Dhaka, but think about now if a river moved across the city. There are so many other pressing problems that the possibility of an earthquake is not high on their radar.

JT It might solve their infrastructure problems...but because of the human costs, to clear that slate would be catastrophic.

SK If we talk about the history of cities–the great Chicago fire, the great fire of London–they were all opportunities to rebuild cities. Historically, city building so often happened at points in time when there were catastrophes.

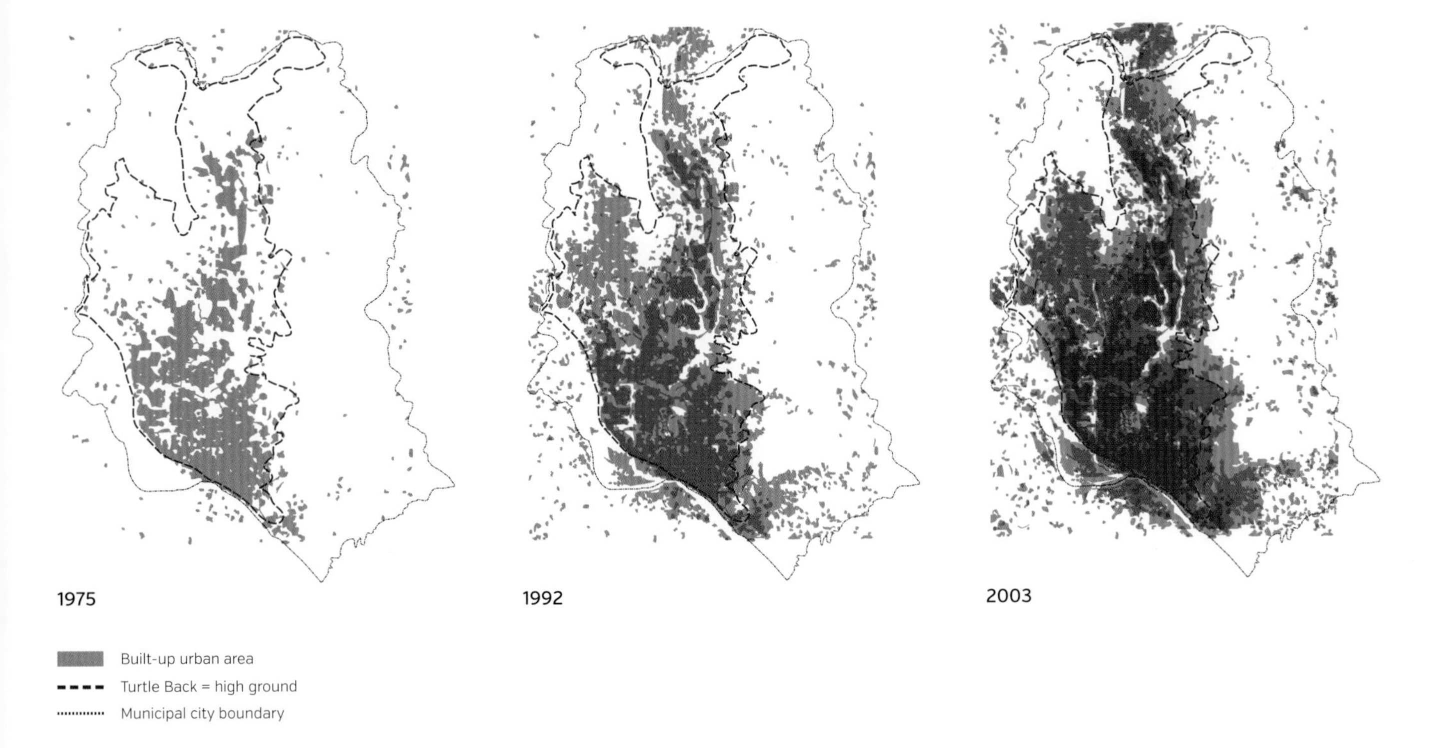

Top: Dhaka is the most densely populated city in the world.

Bottom: Dhaka's urban area has exceeded the limits of the higher-ground and more-stable clay zone known as the "Turtle Back" and is now being built on sand.

+ The Dhaka research lab sought to erase disciplinary boundaries, yet architecture and engineering have dominated Dhaka. How do you think the city's evolution would have differed if led by landscape architects? What role do you think landscape architects have in shaping the city's future?

SK We, for sure, try desperately to involve other disciplines in this context. While running the studio, the area we were most successful in was drawing landscape architecture students to the studio. The disappointment for me, and I think for James, is that we were less successful with other disciplines. We couldn't break through with planning and urban design; even involving engineers from the School of Engineering was very difficult. Did those vantages make a huge difference to how all of us thought about Dhaka? Yes. I think the landscape perspectives were huge and I think the architects started to think like landscape architects in many instances, and everybody started to think like planners to some degree. Some folks started to think like business people. The problem of Dhaka is one that starts to dissolve boundaries a bit naturally because anybody that goes and looks at it as a thinking human being starts to think outside their own personal boundaries.

JT I think you have to take Dhaka and Bangladesh out of it. This isn't about leading, it's about how collaboration can work and about how even collaboration is led. So if you put architects, landscape architects, planners, urban designers, and cultural anthropologists together, depending on who in that group of people is a natural leader–a definer of the query–an agitator towards solving the problem is naturally going to draw the reactive forces from those others in that group towards solving the problem. If you back up for a second and redefine your question through the lens of, if this studio was a landscape architecture studio that happened to have architects in it, I don't think the outcomes would have been different because depending upon the agitation of the architects you would have had more architectural problems. I think it's taking off the cap of being an architect leader for a second and just looking at the question more magnanimously.

SK One of the great virtues of it was that we started to move back to where we began – it's all design of the environment and yes they're disciplines within it but it doesn't mean we can't think outside of our discipline.

JT But I think to be frank, and without naming a project, the projects that we're consultants to as architects–not leading the project but being led by another discipline–have different foci, then we as architects agitate to bring other things to it and vice-versa. If we are leading it, I would hope that the engineers or the landscape architects or the business people would agitate and instigate to broaden the focus of what we are solving.

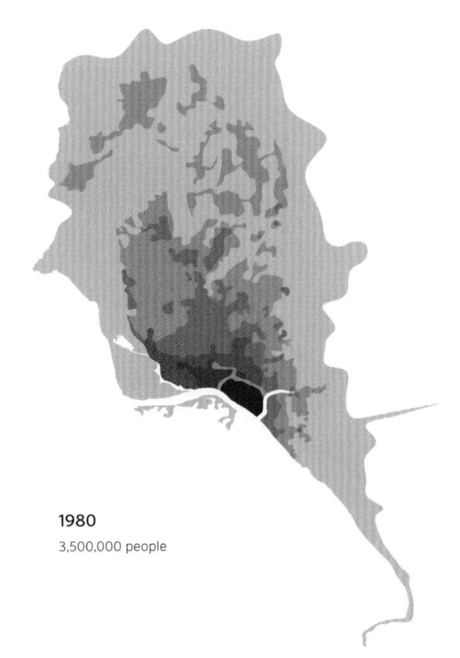

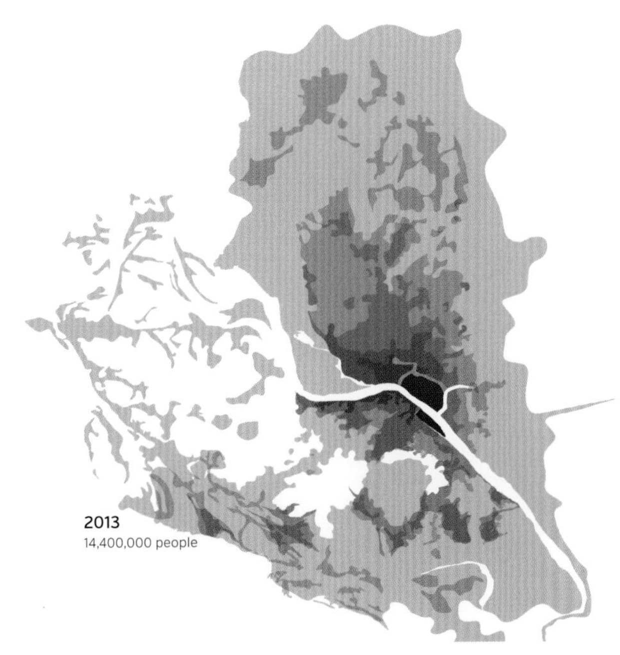

+ In the last chapter of *Alluvium*, you predicted that in the year 2040, "for the poor of Dhaka, little has changed." What role does design have in a city where the primary concerns are social justice, poverty, and health care?

JT That statement was simply stating reality. That idealistically, yes–as an architect, opportunist, and optimist–one would hope that architecture and landscape and social and political changes will elevate people out of that realm. The problem in both Bangladesh and India–and to some degree even in China and the United States–is that there is an institutionalized underclass that is not being addressed. Look at the coal miners in West Virginia and the agitation over taking away the one economic lifeline that they might have. But they are not leaving West Virginia - it is all they know. That Appalachian underclass is continuously underserved and overlooked even as our cities become more gleaming. Philadelphia has never been better in certain areas of the city in the last 45 years than it is now. Yet, you go up to pockets of North Philadelphia and certain parts of southwest Philadelphia and there is still–by birth, by race, by political oppression–an underclass that some people find their way out of and some people don't. I think it was a realistic statement. I think it would have been untrue to write that any other way. People are born into poverty and born into that circumstance but, by the grace of God, you and Steve and I were born into different circumstances. There are those who work their way out of it, there is no question about that, because they are presented opportunities, because they are industrious, they sweep every floor in the world until they work their way out. Given the scale of the population of Dhaka and Bangladesh there are populations that just simply can't get to that '10th block beyond.' It's in New York too, no matter how prosperous it looks. When I read books by architects and urban designers that profess anything other than that...you can't hold that up to the light. It's not truth.

SK The world has always had poverty. Will we see it eradicated in Dhaka? We probably won't see it eradicated in the United States let alone Bangladesh in the next 25 years.

SPEED

ROBERT OLSHANSKY

Robert Olshansky is Professor and Head of the Department of Urban and Regional Planning, University of Illinois at Urbana-Champaign. His research covers post-disaster recovery planning, planning and policy for earthquake risks,hillside planning, and landslide policy. Over the past two decades he has studied recovery planning and management after major disasters in the US, China, Japan, Taiwan, Indonesia, India, and Haiti.

+ PLANNING, GOVERNANCE

Left: Tsunami protection wall at Hamaoka Nuclear Power Station, Japan.

Originally trained as a geologist, I have been an urban and environmental planner for nearly four decades specializing in planning for natural hazards and reconstructing in their wake. I entered this field as an admirer of Ian McHarg. As a student of geomorphology it was nice to think that by listening to the earth it would be easy to identify the suitable places to build. But, after just a few months in planning school in California, it became clear that what works in Pennsylvania might not work in California, where the earth was telling us not to build on hillsides, floodplains, coastal wetlands, prime agricultural lands, critical habitat areas, or areas without water sources.

Perhaps because of my geological training, the one aspect of 'designing with nature' that I retained was the principle of avoiding places that pose hazards to human settlements. Surely, one way we could readily apply environmental science to land use planning would be by mapping natural hazards and regulating development accordingly. This made the most sense for flood hazards, and, in fact, with the advent of the National Flood Insurance Program in 1968 the US was well on its way to mapping the 100-year and 500-year flood zones, forbidding new development in floodways and requiring elevation of all new structures in flood hazard areas. It also made sense to prohibit new development in landslide risk areas, though landslides required more nuanced methods of mapping and regulation than did floodplains. The 1970s also saw the advent in California of the Alquist-Priolo zones, which required special geological studies before construction works in active earthquake fault zones. And the then-new requirement for seismic safety elements in California General Plans was the main vehicle for this optimism that we could use scientific rational planning to identify and design for the most hazardous parts of the landscape. On a national scale, the country was divided into several broad zones of seismic hazard, which formed the basis of building codes to prevent deadly collapse of buildings from expected levels of earthquake shaking. All of these policies had implementation challenges, but the map-and-regulate approach was generally appropriate as a way of guiding new development in the US context.

The one blind side to this approach was that it could not easily solve the problems of pre-existing development in the hazard zones. The National Flood Insurance Program not only accepted the reality of pre-existing structures, but also offered them discounted insurance policies, an unfortunate practice that still continues. Homes in active landslide areas in California had the opportunity to tax themselves to pay for abatement actions, but the expense was a frequent obstacle. Buildings constructed prior to current seismic codes have been a longstanding challenge on the West Coast, and have been the subject of many politically charged debates over the years, primarily because no one wants to absorb the costs of strengthening them.

If one takes a long-term perspective, however, there is a feasible and effective way to address pre-existing hazards: fix them *after* the next natural disaster. We can elevate low-lying buildings after they are flooded, reconstruct new buildings after earthquakes damage them, prohibit reconstruction once landslides occur, and turn hurricane-damaged coastlines into parklands. The surest way to address pre-existing hazards is to completely relocate communities that are in known hazardous areas, and this becomes much easier to accomplish–financially and politically–once a disaster has destroyed them. Following the 1964 Alaskan earthquake, for example, the town of Valdez–destroyed by a tsunami–was completely relocated to a better-protected site a few miles away. The town's residents could retain their fishing-related livelihoods, and the stores and government offices could continue to provide jobs and serve the needs of residents.

However, because people have historic, cultural, or economic reasons for living in specific locations, relocation is not always the best answer. My work in post-disaster reconstruction over the past two decades has taken me to many places in the world where relocations–rationally based on scientific assessments of natural hazards–were not necessarily the most beneficial way to improve the lives of residents. While providing safety from the natural hazard, relocations may in fact have the perverse effect of disrupting lives to the detriment of public health.

This is particularly so where people's livelihoods are closely tied to place. For example, in the Indian state of Tamil Nadu following the great tsunami of 2004, residents within 200 meters of the shore were given free houses in inland locations. But many residents refused to move because the local fishing economy required them to stay close to the sea where they kept their boats and tended their nets. After severe eruptions of Merapi volcano in Indonesia in 2010, the government offered to relocate nearly 80,000 people who were in areas covered by flows of volcanic ash or exposed to future flows. Although some still have unburied fields, most relocated households have had to give up their traditional farming occupations and develop other livelihoods. A 2004 earthquake in the Chuetsu area of Japan caused landslides that affected the lives of residents of numerous mountain villages in this remote, aging, and depopulating part of rural Japan. One of the two affected municipalities encouraged relocation out of the mountains, and the other promoted reconstruction in place. In the end, most households made their decisions based on their own livelihood needs: whether they preferred the agricultural lifestyle in the mountains or chose to provide their family members with access to the modern economy in the urban areas.

Emotional and cultural attachments to place also affect reconstruction decisions. In the town of Kesennuma, Japan, following the 2011 tsunami, residents have resisted the construction of a seawall, a project that would cut off the close connection between the center of town and its fishing harbor. Residents are well aware of the risk, having survived the 2011 event, but they still prioritize their attachment to the sea. Together with government, they are currently working

on a compromise for a levee designed to retain a relationship between the town center and the water. Finally, after 2009's Typhoon Morakot in Southern Taiwan, the government designated dozens of villages as hazardous and provided over 3,000 new residences in 39 relocation sites outside of the mountain areas. These relocation sites are now fully occupied, but villagers are still struggling to define a new equilibrium between their livelihoods, lifestyles, culture, and the inherent risks of living in steep mountains subject to typhoons and landslides.

Although the relationship between livelihood and place is perhaps less significant in the US, people still resist relocation even in the face of obvious natural hazards. For example, people still live in the small coastal community of La Conchita, California, despite experiencing a deadly landslide in 2005 and the continuing threat of future landslide events. And although the enormous Portuguese Bend landslide in southern California has been moving continuously for six decades, people still live atop it, periodically relevelling their homes after significant movements. On a much larger scale, when the state of Louisiana offered over 40,000 Katrina-damaged homeowners in New Orleans the choice to take federal funds to either rebuild in place or sell their flood-damaged property back to the state, 89.5% chose to rebuild. In the long run, such choices might actually reduce overall community risks. We have learnt much from these examples about the importance of social resilience - the ability of some communities to adapt to natural hazards and survive disasters regardless of the quantitatively measured objective risk.

Planning and design of new developments must incorporate our knowledge of natural hazards and cost-effective methods of reducing the risks of future disasters. But when existing developments are in places that we now know to be hazardous, the solutions are not so obvious. People have reasons for living where they do, and relocating them–in addition to being costly–can create unintended negative effects. It is tempting to think that disasters create a 'blank map' similar to undeveloped land, but property rights, social ties, and cultural attachments to place mean this is not so. Instead, we need to think more broadly about risk, incorporating social and economic effects, and taking a public health perspective that considers the long-term effects on households and the lives of residents. When considering post-disaster relocations, we need to balance monetary costs, public safety, and the social and public health risks that could result from all the possible alternative actions.

JON COAFFEE + JONATHAN CLARKE
RESILIENT
URBANISM
2.0

Jon Coaffee is Professor in Urban Geography at the School of Politics and International Studies at the University of Warwick, UK where he runs the Resilient Cities Laboratory. His research focuses upon the interplay of physical and socio-political aspects of urban resilience, including the impact of risk on the functioning of urban areas. Coaffee is the author of six books, the most recent being *Urban Resilience: Planning for Risk, Crisis and Uncertainty* (2016). His work has been supported by a number of EU and UK Research Council grants.

Jonathan Clarke is a Post-Doctoral Research Fellow in the Resilient Cities Laboratory at the University of Warwick. His work considers the roles of design, planning, and governance in identifying and responding to future urban challenges with a particular focus upon comparative, international security arrangements. He is an experienced urban designer, planner, and landscape architect, specialising in regeneration, masterplanning, environmental impact assessment, and public realm design. Clarke is a professional practice examiner for the Landscape Institute, UK.

+ URBAN GEOGRAPHY, DESIGN

The need to be adaptable to change and cope with growing risk, disruption, and volatility–to be *resilient*–is seen as perhaps the most urgent challenge of our time. While not geared toward any single shock or stress, resilience is a part of a process which recognizes that the future is going to be considerably different from the past and that in order to survive and thrive we need to radically change current approaches. Learning to adapt in pursuit of greater resilience provides an antidote to the unpredictability of our future world and is becoming increasingly central to redesigning urban life in the 21st century.

Today, ideas of resilience present different viewpoints that allow us to see the future afresh. In the recent past, ideas of reducing vulnerability through risk management have dominated discussions on how society can control the future. Whilst these conventional approaches helped us prepare and plan for disruption and to 'bounce back,' new approaches promote the need to anticipate future challenges and enhance the capacity to adapt: in essence to 'bounce forwards.'

Coping with Persistent Risk and Uncertainty

Human imagination is becoming increasingly driven by the possibility of surprise or 'black swan' events–low probability but high impact 'shocks'–that have dramatic, far-reaching effects on both localities and global society. Most starkly, the risk of large-scale terrorist attack against urban areas has expanded significantly since the events of 9/11 leading to an increased requirement for security considerations to be an integral part of the design and planning process. The speed of urbanization over the last few decades has also shaped the threat environment in which urban terrorism has evolved, with attacks less predictable but with increased consequences given the domino effects of disruption of one urban infrastructure on others. In 2015 alone, Europol–the European Union's law enforcement agency–reported that there were over 200 failed, foiled, and completed terrorist attacks in the EU. Most notably, attacks against 'soft' public spaces–crowded locations where people gather–have also necessitated that design becomes part of the security process and that interventions be proportionate to the risk faced. We want our urban areas to be safe but we don't necessarily want them looking like fortresses. Built environment professionals involved in public space design are now increasingly working alongside dedicated security planners and the initial swathe of security barriers that littered the landscape of many Western cities in the wake of 9/11 are giving way to more subtle alterations in urban design that seek to balance the need to provide effective physical security with aesthetic and social impacts of these measures.

Concomitantly to terrorist risk we inhabit a new climatic norm that has seen a dramatic increase in weather-related catastrophes, such as floods, storms, and drought.[1] In the UK, flooding in the winter of 2015/16 saw over 3,500 homes flooded and 8,000 more left without power, highlighting the continuing failure to accommodate flooding in the planning of new developments and critical infrastructure. In May and June 2016, there was major flooding across Europe – most notably in Paris where the Seine reached its highest level since 1955. All of this pales in comparison to the recent flooding of the South Indian states of Tamil Nadhu and Andhra, in 2015 which are believed to have killed over 500 people and left a further 1.8 million displaced from their homes. If this sounds familiar, it is probably because the remarkable increase in these mega-disasters have starkly highlighted the requirement for enhanced resilience, as well as the failings of earlier development regimes. This is especially crucial as, by the latest estimates, there are one billion people living on land vulnerable to flooding globally – a figure that will rise to two billion by 2050, with the cities of the developing world being particularly vulnerable.[2]

In recent decades the world has moved into a more dangerous and unpredictable [geological] epoch; the Anthropocene presents a new challenge for humanity, operating in a harsher and more volatile world of "persistent uncertainty."[3] A key motif of the Anthropocene is that what we consider 'normal' is changing and that the future has become increasingly difficult to predict. In evidence of this, when Hurricane Sandy hit New York in 2012 it was considered to be a one-in-one-hundred-year event, but more recent research indicates that events of a similar magnitude could potentially occur as frequently as one in every four years by 2070.[4]

The Promise of Resilient Design

The 'resilience turn' in the early 2000s saw resilience approaches embedded within an array of global initiatives, national policies, and local practices. Despite the often contested understanding of resilience, there is a growing consensus that resilience can be understood as the capacity to withstand and rebound from a range of disruptive challenges, considered through the lens of an evolving range of contemporary risks, and as part of an ongoing process of change and transformation. Nowhere is such modification more prominent than in the design and redesign of cities. Events such as extreme flooding or large-scale terror attack increasingly challenge the legitimacy of technical and traditional engineered approaches to hazard mitigation and the quantitative basis of conventional risk management. It is here that resilient design approaches have emerged as a way of extending risk management approaches and moving beyond traditional technical solutions to more proactive, adaptive, and everyday applications within the built environment.

Recent research suggests that urban disasters often result from failures in city design and that an understanding of these failures holds the key to new forms of resilient design that engage with the complexities of the urban medium and the uncertainty of future threats in a comprehensive manner.[5]

These complex problems are difficult for any single profession to address in isolation. Consequently, we are seeing the advancement of holistic, design-based approaches that offer innovative and forward-thinking solutions to elevated risk and rising uncertainty, forging new relationships between the built environment and critical infrastructure, as well as an expanding range of professional practices. It is this capacity for change that fundamentally interlinks landscape and the urban medium. Infrastructure should no longer be considered a component within the urban landscape, rather it is the landscape that is the predominant infrastructure of the urban system and its design and management requires integrated practice.

This is, however, far from a straightforward task and until recently there has been a noticeable implementation gap in resilient design practice. Too much of our built environment is maladaptive; that is, design that is no longer fit for purpose, has reached functional obsolescence, and increases wider vulnerability. Furthermore, development norms are habitually shaped by professional siloes, with engineers and technical disciplines overseeing quantitative risk management, and architects, planners, and landscape architects brought in to address specific design problems. These separated practices are too often 'locked-in' by the awkward arrangements over legal and professional accountabilities, limiting holistic approaches, the ability to learn from past events, or to provide new approaches that meet the emerging issues of the day. As Dick Wright, chair of the American Society of Civil Engineers' Sustainable Infrastructure Education committee, has noted, "[t]oday's design criteria and codes are built on the weather of the past – this is the challenge."[6]

Practicing Resilient Design

Resilient design represents a progressive agenda for urban development by bringing together hazard mitigation and design in both systems and infrastructure at the citywide scale, where disaster events can be catalytic and reshape professional design practice. Risk trends amplify the pressure upon cities to keep citizens safe, healthy, prosperous, well informed, and supplied with essential services, yet to date a comprehensive approach to improve the resilience and security of large-scale urban development against disruptions has not been thoroughly developed. Filling this gap was the overarching aim of HARMONISE – an EU-funded research project[7] that developed a multi-faceted approach for enhancing the resilience and sustainability of urban infrastructure. The project's goal was to improve decision-making amongst a range of built environment professionals across the design and planning phases of development projects, illuminating the need for holistic thinking in order to create a more resilient urban future.

Urban resilience, if operationalized effectively, can provide a practical explanatory framework for urban design practitioners seeking to work with risk, crisis, and uncertainty and genuinely transform the way in which they work. Here significant cultural

change requires the interweaving of principles of resilience into the everyday repertoires of urban practice. It should become a consideration in everything built environment professionals do across the different parts of the design and planning process – from initial concept design of development schemes and the granting of planning permission, through to construction and, importantly, monitoring and maintenance of the built environment. Ideally this should be a process of utilizing resilience as everyday practice rather than a compliance-based approach using regulation and statutory codes of practice. Blending the planning lifecycle with the resilience cycle of mitigation, response, and recovery in a continuous and dynamic way, although challenging, would significantly assist the advancement of holistic urban resilience concepts and practice.

By way of example, we can point to schemes across Europe that are now embodying the principles of resilient design in response to a range of risks. In Copenhagen, a masterplan led by SLA architects uses the need to alleviate localized flood risk from 'cloudburst' rain events as an opportunity for advancing a series of coherent public spaces that provide a range of co-benefits.[8] A network of sunken basins with water-purifying plantings utilize a range of natural processes to provide greater rainwater catchment to alleviate flooding, but the design also offers a vibrant range of community uses to improve the residents' quality of life. This beautiful parkland setting both deals with anticipated urban risk while also contributing to wider social, cultural, and environmental quality, and an increasing awareness of local climate change issues.

In London, urban designers and landscape architects have been involved in advancing more aesthetically appealing features for mitigating terrorist risk. Such advances range from streetscape elements that camouflage their intent as hostile vehicle mitigation barriers (maximizing 'stand-off' distance to any targeted area) to whole site design. For example, recent public-realm streetscape improvements in central London have seen more-attractive and inconspicuous security features designed in the form of balustrades. Likewise, the new Emirates Stadium in North London has actively promoted its ornamental counter-terrorism features, consisting of large concrete letters spelling out Arsenal, the resident football club. These are held up as a model of best practice for designing for counter-terrorism.[9]

At a whole-of-site level the current plans for the new US Embassy in southwest London have sought to incorporate a number of innovative and largely stealthy counter-terrorism design features.[10] Architects KieranTimberlake stated that the design had been inspired by "European castle" architecture and that, in addition to the blast-proof glass facade, landscape features such as ponds and multi-level gardens are used imaginatively as security devices to minimize the use of fences and walls to avoid a "fortress" development.[11] The embassy design highlights a number of key features of contemporary counter-terrorism philosophy including the need to integrate effective protective security into the design of sites at risk; the increased importance of built environment professionals such as planners, landscape architects, and urban designers in security planning; and the need to consider the visible impact of security measures and, where appropriate, make these as unobtrusive as possible.[12]

A further example of resilient design in practice can be elucidated from the national approach in the Netherlands which is embedding principles of 'water' or 'blue' planning into everyday design practice with the aim of reducing potential risks and enhancing the resilience of the built environment. Adopted in February 2010, the nationwide Delta Program promotes a philosophy known as Adaptive Delta Management (ADM), which requires designers to be more anticipative of the future conditions and challenges of climate change. Using a scenario matrix that looks at the links between climate change and socio-economic development, ADM develops a range of "adaptation pathways" as an alternative to the traditional end-point scenario, explicitly acknowledging the uncertainty in climate change.[13] Here multiple scenarios are used to anticipate a range of options, leaving room for emergent policy processes and outcomes.

The proactive Dutch ADM program is in its infancy but its holistic, adaptive, pragmatic, flexible, and anticipatory philosophy of design has seen the approach utilized around the world, notably in Bangladesh, Indonesia, and Vietnam, but also in New Orleans where the *Dutch Dialogues*—a series of US-Dutch workshops—helped shape the post-Katrina comprehensive water management strategy. As opposed to the overly technical and single purpose design of the past, the approach is formulated through a series of local workshops as part of a collaborative, iterative design process, which use learning and adaptation to overcome potential implementation gaps.

These examples from Copenhagen, London, and the Netherlands provide us with vital lessons from Europe illustrating how design approaches can overcome the implementation gap in resilience practice. Foremost is the need to anticipate, mitigate, and manage risks and vulnerabilities; in practice this will involve an ongoing relationship with risk, rather than earlier approaches that 'design out' risks, typically involving the construction of bigger walls or military security design.[14] Better education and training is also of crucial importance to foster holistic and adaptive approaches. For resilient design to be effective, built environment professions cannot function in isolation and must be part of a more-integrated urban management nexus, raising awareness of options that are available to *all* built environment professionals involved in the decision-making process. Here, allowing adaptive capacity skills to be forged in a multidisciplinary and multi-professional environment, mirroring the complex reality of urban resilience problems on the ground, is vital.

1 See Thomas Fisher, *Designing to Avoid Disaster: The Nature of Fracture-Critical Design* (London: Routledge, 2012).

2 UN-HABITAT, *Cities and Climate Change: Global Report on Human Settlements* (London: Earthscan, 2011).

3 Frank Biermann, "The Anthropocene: A Governance Perspective," *The Anthropocene Review* 1, no. 1 (2014): 58.

4 New York State Energy Research and Development Authority, *Responding to Climate Change in New York State: The ClimAID Integrated Assessment for Effective Climate Change Adaptation in New York State* (New York: Blackwell Publishing, 2011).

5 Fisher, *Designing to Avoid Disaster*.

6 Cited in Jared Green, "Preparing for Climate Change," *The Dirt* (2016) https://dirt.asla.org/2016/05/24/how-to-plan-and-design-in-a-changing-climate/ (accessed July 5, 2016).

7 HARMONISE (Holistic Approach to Resilience and Systematic Actions to Make Large Scale Built Infrastructure Secure) is a project which has received funding from the European Union's Seventh Framework Program for research, technological development and demonstration. See www.harmonise.eu.

8 See Hans Tavsens Park and Korsgade by SLA Architects, Denmark http://www.sla.dk/en/projects/hanstavsenspark (accessed December 20, 2016).

9 Jon Coaffee, Paul O'Hare & Marian Hawkesworth, "The Visibility of (In)security: The Aesthetics of Planning Urban Defences Against Terrorism," *Security Dialogue* 40 (2009): 489–511.

10 See http://www.kierantimberlake.com/pages/view/88/embassy-of-the-united-states-of-america/parent:3 (accessed September 7, 2016).

11 "Ambassador, you are spoiling our view of the Thames with this boring glass cube," *The Guardian* (February 23, 2010), https://www.theguardian.com/uk/2010/feb/23/us-ambassador-spoiling-view-embassy.

12 Jon Coaffee, "Protecting Vulnerable Cities: The UK Resilience Response to Defending Everyday Urban Infrastructure," *International Affairs* 86, no. 4 (2010): 939–54.

13 Jon Coaffee & Peter Lee, *Urban Resilience: Planning for Risk, Crisis and Uncertainty* (London: Palgrave, 2016).

14 Jon Coaffee & Jonathan Clarke, "On Securing the Generational Challenge of Urban Resilience," *Town Planning Review* 86, no. 3, (2015): 249–55.

Previous Page: SLA's masterplan for Inner Nørrebro, Copenhagen employs nature-based design strategies to alleviate flood risk.

Opposite: KieranTimberlake's design for a new US Embassy in London utilizes landscape features as security devices.

JACKY BOWRING

EXTREME LANDSCAPES
A 21ST CENTURY SUBLIME

Dr Jacky Bowring is Professor of Landscape Architecture at Lincoln University, Christchurch, New Zealand. Her research uses methods of design, critique, and scholarship, and delves into areas of landscape, memory, and emotion. She is author of *A Field Guide to Melancholy* (2008) and *Melancholy and the Landscape* (2016), and is editor of *Landscape Review*.

+ DESIGN, CULTURAL STUDIES

Dangling, upside down, by a rope. Suspended in a chasm. Pure fear, delicious. Here is Shelley's "Dizzy Ravine,"[1] and Coleridge's "precipitous, black, jagged rock."[2] All of those Romantic visions of terror and torrents, the sublime delight in the landscape's extremes. But this is far from the grand tourists wandering through Europe. This is Queenstown, New Zealand.

Trembling, awe-struck, in a devastated city. The ground in turmoil. Death and destruction. Like Captain O'Hara's "awful yet tremendous scene" on viewing Lisbon after the 1755 earthquake.[3] Or Charles Darwin's witnessing of the 1835 Chilean earthquake and reporting the "most awful yet interesting spectacle."[4] This is Christchurch, New Zealand.

Queenstown and Christchurch are twin poles of New Zealand's landscape of risk. As the country's 'adventure capital,' Queenstown is a spectacular landscape in which risk is a commodity. Christchurch's landscape is also risky, ruptured by earthquakes, tentatively rebuilding. As a far-flung group of tiny islands in a vast ocean, New Zealand is the poster-child of the sublime. Through the eyes of the European artists of the 18th and 19th centuries, this landscape offered up sublimity in its mountains, lakes, waterfalls, glaciers, and fiords – a microcosmic Grand Tour. Themes of remoteness,[5] solitude,[6] danger, beauty, and drama resonate throughout its short history, and were underlined by the imagining of New Zealand as Tolkein's "Middle Earth."[7]

For Queenstown, the sublime drives an industry that runs on danger. It's the place for an "adrenaline rush," and home to "the latest and greatest adventure activities, there are Queenstown adrenaline activities for every thrill seeker, from iconic Queenstown bungee jumping to whitewater rafting, river surfing, canyon swinging and thrills on a jet boat. Queenstown has it all!"[8] The sublime has burst out of its 18th-century frame and is no longer held at arm's length, but plunged into. Aesthetics, after all, embraces much more than the merely visual; it was, as literary theorist Terry Eagleton explained, "born as a discourse of the body."[9]

Queenstown's sublime builds on its spectacular setting, and wrings out of this landscape as much as possible in terms of a theatrical performance of risk. For designers, the sublime drives challenges: to maximize the awe, to dangle the tourist further over the abyss, or propel them faster through the maelstrom. Queenstown's endless appetite for thrills ripples out through the landscape, testing designers not just to be infinitely innovative in tourist experiences, but also to increase access into the landscape. A monorail, gondola, and tunnel have all been proposed as ways of getting tourists further into the wilderness. And in 2016, $18 million was spent for additional lights and runway widening to allow night flights to bring in even more adventure tourists to Queenstown.

Improved access highlights the paradox of the 21st-century sublime. It is increasingly possible for anyone to enter into this truly dangerous landscape. The terrain around Queenstown is treacherous, an extreme landscape of avalanches and alpine conditions. Beyond the managed risk of commercial thrills, the proximity of extreme landscapes makes the danger very real – and increasing access amplifies the situation. Already it is possible to drive your car very close to glaciers, mountains, and wild rivers, get out and go for a walk. Recently a mother and daughter visiting from the United States went out for a walk, and ended up being rescued days later, "just hours from death." The risk that comes with going for a walk is not the spectacular theatrics of dicing with death that drives "muscular tourism"[10] such as whitewater rafting, bungee jumping, and skydiving. In a sublime landscape, death can come from the simple act of getting lost.

Risk's significant other–safety–tethers New Zealand's 21st-century sublime. The experiencing of fear in Queenstown is something of a sleight of hand, a carefully orchestrated plummet into the unknown, with a precise dose of adrenalin. The theatrics are played out as a pseudo-sublime, gently cushioned by legislation. New Zealand's health and safety regulations respond to a legacy of adventure tourism deaths, alongside the high fatality rates in risky industries like mining and forestry. In the decade 2004 to 2014, 63 overseas tourists died in adventure tourism accidents in New Zealand, and tourism operators are very aware that deaths are bad for business.

While Queenstown pushes the envelope into higher and faster thrills, Christchurch's sublime is not a consumer product. Shaken apart by a series of earthquakes beginning in September 2010, the city's relationship with its landscape is one of awe and respect. As resident Gail Dowgray observed, "In a way it's quite magnificent looking at those cliffs. It is quite a magnificent sight what Mother Nature did to us."[11] Christchurch is not in the hunt for endless thrills, but a kind of equilibrium, a stabilizing and recuperation. Here the dimension of aesthetics is bound to the idea of dwelling, of being-in-the-world, and an ethic of care.

Christchurch's design response draws deeply on the sublime's origins. While Queenstown's sublime is tempered by health and safety legislation, in Christchurch it finds a conscience through the frame of empathy. The sublime is fraught with paradox, including the tension between danger and delight. Finding pleasure in the spectacle of destruction became recognized as morally wrong, including in Ruskin's recognition of the "heartlessness" of images of suffering.[12] Empathy and caring provide a balance, an antidote; some of the first examples of aid and compassion coming from far afield were experienced with the 1755 Lisbon earthquake, a "global, imagined empathy with the sufferings of distant strangers."[13]

The upwelling of empathy, care, and rehabilitation has brought surprising emotional responses for Christchurch, a city previously known for its conservatism and reserve. Residents vehemently expressed their love for the landscape, even the places that had killed some of the 185 earthquake victims. As Christchurch now goes about rebuilding a city where over 80% of the central business district was lost–and re-imagining parts of the city that can't be rebuilt, such as the residential red zone where 8,000 homes have since been demolished–design is carefully attuned to risk. Design is seen as restorative, both literally in terms of physical fabric, as well as in the spirit of the city and the well-being of its residents. Amidst the inevitable debates over the politics of the rebuild, there are many exemplars of the potency of temporary landscapes, and their vital place as moments of joy.

The importance of participation was underscored by the Christchurch City Council's Share An Idea project, which gathered 106,000 ideas to inspire the city's rebuild.[14] The 48-Hour Design Challenge, Gap Filler (which develops temporary art spaces), Greening the Rubble (which focuses on temporary landscapes), and Life in Vacant Spaces (which matches community initiatives with available sites) are just a few of the design-focused responses to the post-quake city. And just as risk mitigation is formalized in the adventure tourism industry through health and safety regulations, the earthquakes forced dramatic changes to New Zealand's building codes. Commissions of inquiry and coronial inquests into Christchurch's building collapses have heightened the awareness of construction and compliance issues, and as a negative consequence many heritage and character buildings around the country are being demolished because it is not economically viable to bring them up to required standards.

Queenstown and Christchurch tell two different, yet complementary, stories about the sublime. Queenstown rushes headlong into embracing the sublimity of its landscape, augmenting it, amplifying it, selling it. This is risk as entertainment. Alongside the leaping, flying, jumping, skiing, and biking, are some of New Zealand's most exclusive restaurants, hotels, and boutiques. All of this built on a legacy of the paradoxical intersection of fear and pleasure. Christchurch's story is a reminder of the ethical dimension of the sublime. At the same time as landscape's danger can be a spectacle, there must also be a consideration for humanity, for the trauma experienced by those thrust into the middle of the events. Restoring and rebuilding happens amidst the ongoing fear, the knowledge that this might not be over, as the city still trembles with over 14,000 aftershocks.

Christchurch and Queenstown are vehicles for exploring the 21st-century sublime, for reflecting on its expansive influence on shaping cultural landscapes. Transcending the affectations of Shelley, Coleridge, Captain O'Hara, and Darwin, New Zealand's 21st-century sublime is vivid and immersive. Pushing at the thresholds of safety and risk, Queenstown is a place for designers to play. It is a place of innovation: this is where the bungee jump was invented, and the jetboat was developed nearby. And in Christchurch, the previously reserved and unemotional city has become a place where residents regularly have their say and have become active participants in debates about urban design and architecture. Risk drives innovation in Christchurch too, with internationally renowned seismic engineering alongside quirky and temporary experimental landscapes that nimbly negotiate the constantly changing context. Christchurch and Queenstown stretch and challenge the sublime's influence on the designed landscape. Circling the paradoxes of risk and safety, suffering and pleasure, the sublime feeds an infinite appetite for fear as entertainment, and at the same time calls for an empathetic caring for a broken landscape and its residents.

Right: Damage to Christchurch Cathedral following the 2011 earthquakes.

1 Percy Bysshe Shelley, "Mont Blanc" [1817] cited in Cian Duffy, *Shelley and the Revolutionary Sublime* [Cambridge: Cambridge University Press, 2005], 115.

2 Samuel Taylor Coleridge, "Hymn before Sunrise" [1802] cited in Sally West, *Coleridge and Shelley: Textual Engagement* [Abingdon, Oxon: Routledge, 2016], 93.

3 Alexander Regier, *Fracture and Fragmentation in British Romanticism* [Cambridge: Cambridge University Press, 2010], 84.

4 Paul White, "Darwin, Concepción and the Geological Sublime," *Science in Context* 25, no.1 [2012]: 56.

5 Keith Sinclair, *Distance Looks Our Way: The Effect of Remoteness of New Zealand* [Auckland: Paul's Book Arcade, 1961].

6 John Mulgan, *Man Alone* [Auckland: Penguin, 1999, first published 1939].

7 As in Peter Jackson's three *Lord of the Rings* films [2001, 2002, 2003] and three films of The Hobbit [2012, 2013, 2014].

8 "Queenstown Adventure and Adrenaline," http://www.queenstownnz.co.nz/information/adventure-activities/ [accessed September 15, 2016].

9 Terry Eagleton, *The Ideology of the Aesthetic* [London: Wiley-Blackwell, 1990], 13.

10 Tim Edensor points to "the rise of muscular tourism, the proliferating collection of adventurous pursuits based upon white-water rafting, canoeing, mountain-biking, surfing and skateboarding, snowboarding, bungee jumping, hang-gliding, and orienteering have supplemented the older activities of walking, skiing, swimming, and climbing, and have ramped up the values of risk, thrill, and competition." Tim Edensor, "Tourism," in *International Encyclopaedia of Human Geography* [Amsterdam: Elsevier, 2009], 308.

11 "House Doesn't Matter, Says Owner," *The Press* [February 18, 2012] 2.

12 In Malcolm Andrews, *The Picturesque: Literary Sources and Documents*, vol. 1 [Robertsbridge, UK: Helm Information, 1994], 33.

13 Sharon Sliwinski, "The Aesthetics of Human Rights," *Culture, Theory and Critique* 5, no. 1 [2009]: 24.

14 Christchurch is a city of around 400,000 residents, and the response to the project was recognised in the International Co-creation Award https://www.ccc.govt.nz/the-rebuild/strategic-plans/share-an-idea/ [accessed June 26, 2016].

NO RISK, NO PLAY

BERNARD SPIEGAL

Bernard Spiegal is Director of PLAYLINK, a consultancy focused on the creation and maintenance of public and communal outdoor space, encompassing parks, public realm projects, schools, and social and mixed tenure housing. His work is particularly focused on the issues of play and risk. Spiegal is advisor to the UK Play Safety Forum and is co-author of *Children's Play Space and Safety Management: Rethinking the Role of Play Equipment Standards* (2014).

+ DESIGN

Children and teenagers want and need to take risks. They do this 'naturally' in the sense that, left to their own devices, they seek out and create encounters that carry degrees of risk or uncertainty. This process of risk-taking necessarily entails exploration, discovery, and learning – about oneself, one's capabilities, and the wider world. To take a risk is to assert one's autonomy and power of agency. It is to *learn by doing* that actions have consequences. It is an aspect of moral education. Play and risk-taking are creative acts. A perspective to bear in mind as we briefly survey the scene.

Here's a conventional playground: fenced, rubber or synthetic 'safety' surface, inert, uniform, dead. Inside the fence are metal swings, slides, and climbing frames. Climbing, swinging, and sliding are the only actions the equipment formally allows. But there are always renegades who will use equipment 'wrongly' – climbing onto the roof of play equipment that was not 'meant' for climbing, or being upside down on a swing or slide. It's simple really: children are exercising their sense of agency, their autonomy, their creative capacity to bend even seemingly resistant environments to their own purposes and interests. And the risks they take are generated by *their* choices, *their* imaginations, *their* creativity. The designer, weighted with rule book, restrictive (and often questionable) design standards, and liability anxieties may be part of the problem, not the solution.

But perhaps we should start with rights, rather than design. Spatial rights. In this case, the rights of children and teenagers to be able to roam, use, and loiter around their cities, towns, and villages. Their rights to be seen and heard within shared social space. The right to play. And the concomitant requirement on adults not to think those rights are being accommodated simply by the provision of sequestered, age-defined reservations; that is, playgrounds. Simply saying this, thinking this, reframes the way space and its potential is perceived.

Here's a new rule: all design briefs that aim to take account of children, teenagers, and families should prohibit the creation of playgrounds. A salutary benefit here would be to force designers to see the entire environment as potentially available to children. To be effective, this would require adults to nurture sensitivity and insight by noticing what children *actually do*, as distinct from what they may say they like to do when asked in some useless consultation. Recalling one's own childhood can offer clues in this regard. Readers of this are likely to have been children once.

This is not a technical, apolitical exercise. Rather, it is underpinned by a key value: the need to legitimise children in public and communal space. This is risky stuff, given how teenagers in particular are often negatively perceived, and that's without considering perceptions and prejudices in respect of race and class.

Children will always like to swing, slide, climb, and there are many ways to provide those experiences, *one* way being specialist equipment (though it doesn't need to be in a playground). But the wider, more general point is that the environment as a whole has the potential to be playable space. What curtails that potential is a culture of prohibition combined with a uni-perspective, such that a bench is only for sitting, but not for climbing and jumping. Our attention needs to be directed towards engendering a culture of permission along with a broad view of what constitutes 'playability.'

This is not to suggest unhindered licence – there is an etiquette of reciprocal and mutual courtesies to be observed by all users of shared space. But the form and meaning this takes is in part governed by whether a culture of prohibition or permission prevails. Children and teenagers being seen and heard in shared public and communal space is one of the hallmarks of a society at ease with itself. We are not at ease.

Opposite: "The Sad Effects of Climbing Trees" from *The Accidents of Youth*, 1819.

MANAGING RISK IN THE ENERGYSHED

MARK ALAN HUGHES, CORNELIA COLIJN + OSCAR SERPELL

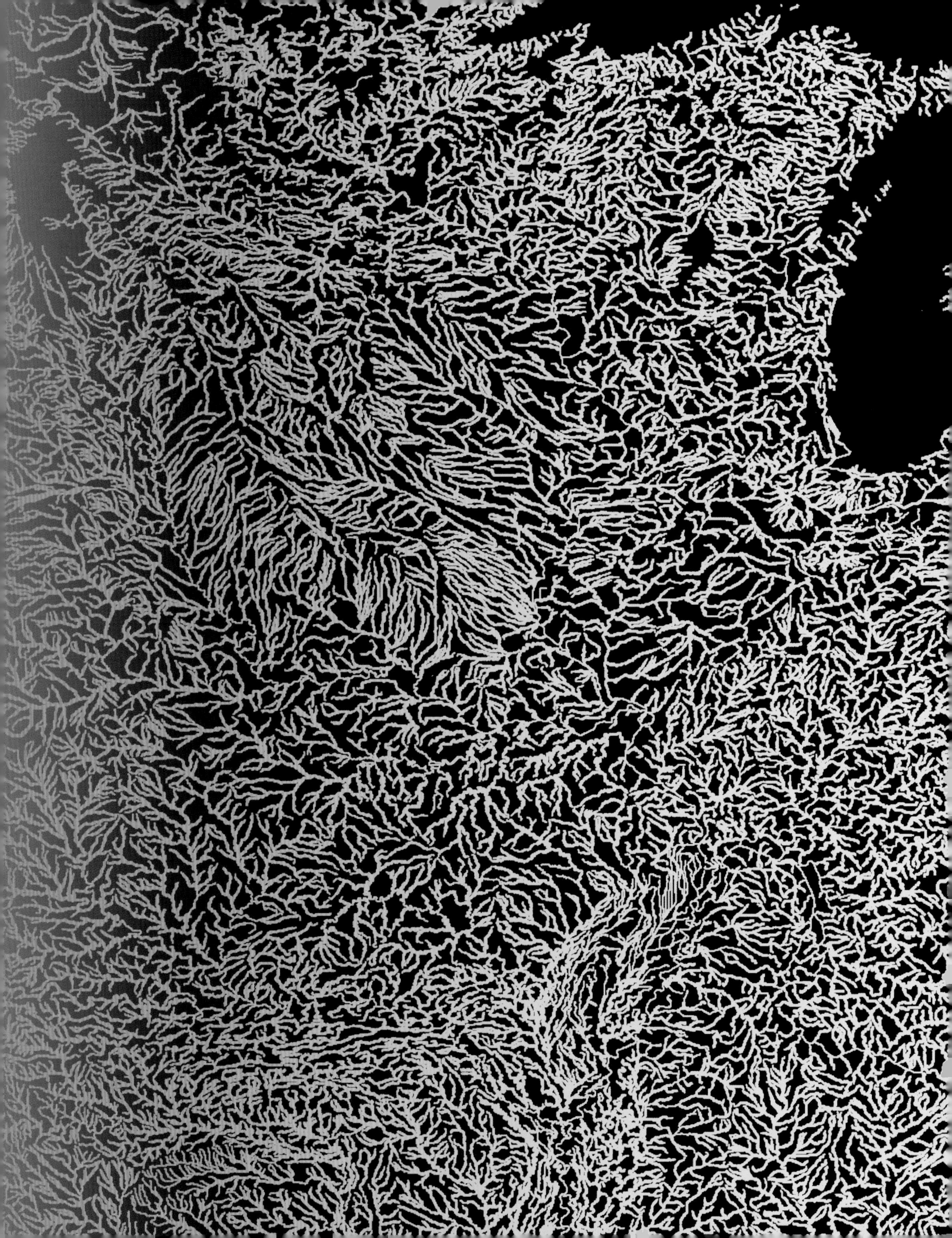

Mark Alan Hughes is a Professor of Practice at the University of Pennsylvania School of Design. He is Founding Director of the Kleinman Center for Energy Policy and Faculty Director of the Fels Policy Research Initiative. Hughes holds a PhD in Regional Science from the University of Pennsylvania.

Cornelia Colijn is the Deputy Director of the Kleinman Center for Energy Policy. She holds a graduate degree in Applied Geosciences from the University of Pennsylvania and teaches in the University's Masters of Environmental Studies program.

Oscar Serpell is a Research Fellow at the Kleinman Center for Energy Policy. He holds a graduate degree in Natural Resource Management from the University of Pennsylvania.

+ ENERGY POLICY, HYDROLOGY, GOVERNANCE

This essay explores the spatial organization of energy systems and suggests that, much like watersheds, certain aspects of energy generation, transmission, distribution, optimization, and consumption are organized at a regional scale that is not well represented by the conventional boundaries of energy policymakers. We label this spatial organization at the regional scale the "energyshed" and suggest that the energy system might be better managed with improved alignment between decision-making and regional energysheds. This prospect is particularly compelling when resource management is seen as a comprehensive strategy to manage risks, especially those risks characterized by the uncertainty of climate change, the prospects for energy security, and the transition to clean energy sources.

The energy system implicates risk beyond relatively direct operational risk of, say, grid failure and resulting blackouts. Decarbonizing our energy sytem is the primary instrument of climate policy, the purpose of which is to reduce the risk of far more indirect events such as flooding and drought. In the examples below, we focus on the electricity sector because decarbonizing electricity is one of the easier energy challenges we face in reducing the emissions that are driving climate change. We are already witnessing natural gas displacing coal in the competitive market; soon renewables are projected to overtake natural gas, which will reduce to near zero the emission profile of electricity production.[1] On the demand side of the energy system, the disruptive change comes from the electrification of the transportation sector. The energy density of gasoline has, up until now, been very hard to displace. But breakthroughs in battery technology have finally made such displacement possible and inceasingly likely over a transition period of several decades.[2]

Our claim in this essay is that without a better alignment between the spatial organization of energy systems and the boundaries of decision-making, the energy system cannot be optimized to meet policy goals such as grid reliability and climate change mitigation. Much like a map of jurisdictional boundaries obscures the boundaries of watersheds, such boundaries also obscure regional energysheds and impede the efficient risk and resource management that energysheds might support. Finding ways to reveal and leverage these regional and local platforms for strategic energy management are important because the energy system is seen as a critical instrument in achieving a number of national and international policy goals ranging from the Sustainable Development Goals to the New Urban Agenda of Habitat III to the Nationally Determined Contributions toward the goals of COP21, commonly referred to as the Paris Agreement.[3]

In this essay, we explore the analogy between watersheds and the proposed energyshed concept. With dynamics similar to watersheds, energysheds internalize costs and benefits in ways that can optimize outcomes in terms of efficiency and equity, and offer a mechanism for energy policymakers to mitigate collective action problems that prevent society from optimizing the benefit of energy services within a regional energyshed.[4]

Watersheds are defined as an area of land, delineated by topographic highs that drain to a common point. Drainage defines watershed boundaries with a clarity that is rarely the case with the boundaries of socially constructed systems with a spatial organization, such as markets or dialects or sporting loyalties. Hydrogeologists can accurately predict groundwater recharge, map floodplains, and trace pollution pathways, all from an understanding of the basic principles of how drainage basins function. This precision and accuracy supports the rational management of watersheds to achieve a social goal such as maximizing the value of water services. As the effects of climate change stress the natural hydrologic cycle, this watershed-level work is increasingly important in informing the management of water resources in a reliable, efficient, and equitable way.

But this management is often confounded by a simple fact: watersheds, and their associated river systems, defy jurisdictional boundaries. If we had heeded the advice of 19th-century geologist and United States Geological Survey Director John Wesley Powell and linked our political borders to watershed boundaries, the "United Watersheds of America" would have unrecognizable state jurisdictions.[5] Jurisdictional boundaries challenge holistic watershed management because the decisions of upstream settlements (such as to withdraw water or discharge pollutants) necessarily impact those downstream. Without watershed-wide coordination and governance, jurisdictions responsible for excessive withdrawals and polluting discharges can capture benefits upstream and pass along the environmemtal and public health costs to downstream jurisdictions.

For example, the 330-mile Delaware River forms a 13,000 square mile watershed and serves as a boundary between four mid-Atlantic states: New York, New Jersey, Pennsylvania, and Delaware.[6] In the first half of the 20th century, the Delaware River was plagued with water supply shortages, serious flooding, severe pollution, and disputes over water allocation. By 1960 the watershed had 43 state agencies, 14 interstate agencies, and 19 federal agencies, all having some level of water resource management responsibility. Not surprisingly, these efforts were often duplicative, overlapping, conflicting, and uncoordinated.[7] In short, it was a management disaster.

Then, in 1961, the four states and the federal government (represented by the US Army Corps of Engineers) signed a compact that formally created the Delaware River Basin Commission. This compact set out to address the pollution and volume risks to the Delaware, recognizing "the water and related resources of the basin as regional assets with vested local, State, and National interests with joint responsibility."[8] For the first time in US history these multiple levels of government combined efforts as equal partners in a river basin planning, development, and regulatory agency.

Since that time, through a structured and comprehensive risk-management strategy, the agency has reduced total pollution budgets, restored critical ecosystems, managed water withdrawals, and reduced drought frequency. Just as importantly, the implementation of this strategy required the agency to do the unprecedented: coordinate local, state, and national interests across the basin and organize around the welfare of the watershed as a single system, effectively restoring the watershed as a jurisdictional boundary with standing among the competing boundaries of local, state, and national interests. Fourteen federal basin compacts to address watershed pollution and/or flood control have been created to date.[9]

We suggest that watersheds provide an incomplete but nevertheless instructive analogy to the energy system's relationship to human settlements at a regional scale. The analogy is instructive; first, because similar to watersheds, regional energy resources and infrastructure often contend with jurisdictional boundaries. Secondly, like watersheds, optimized regional energy systems demand multilevel governance and coordination across jurisdictions. And thirdly, as with the increasing recognition of watershed ecobenefits, governments and market actors are increasingly reliant on cities and regions to achieve a critically important energy transition.

As noted earlier, watersheds are characterized as areas of water drainage created by topography that facilitate the optimization of water services through rational management of withdrawls (demand) and discharges (supply) to mitigate negative environmental impacts caused by diffuse management and responsibility. We define energysheds as areas of energy transfer created by infrastructure that facilitate the optimization of energy services through the rational management of load (demand) and capacity (supply) to achieve similar mitigation of negative environmental impacts caused by diffuse management and responsibility in the energy sector.

The strength of the analogy between watersheds and energysheds can be illustrated by a tale of policy development similar to the history of river basin commissions. The US electric grid has often been called the largest and most complex machine ever constructed.[10] The grid is the physical network of connections that transmits electricity over distances and distributes it within markets to be consumed as energy services, the "hot showers and cold beer"[11] in Amory Lovins' memorable phrase. People don't demand water, they demand water services: their thirst quenched, their bodies cooled, the dirt on their clothes and cars dissolved and rinsed away. In the same way, people don't demand energy, they demand hot showers and cold beers, and all the other things that energy makes possible.

Electricity is a product that must be consumed in the instant it is produced lest the grid become unstable. Thus, the reliability of the grid is a fundamental technical and policy goal of the electric system. Reliability is the capacity to meet demand. The challenge of reliability is exacerbated by the fact that demand is often charactized by peak loads at certain times or days of the year. The essential importance of ensuring that generators can and do dispatch increasing amounts of electricity supply on a hot summer day (especially when a thunderstorm interrupts a key connection in the grid) has fostered a complex system of incentives, technologies, and redundancies.[12]

A simple way to strengthen the the value of energy services is to increase the number and diversity of both generators and consumers. This increased scale would allow excess energy capacity in one place to connect to unmet load in another place via expanded physical and administrative infrastructures. In our analogy to watersheds, this is the equivalent of altering topography (i.e., building a canal) to facilitate new drainage patterns in order to create new value in water services.

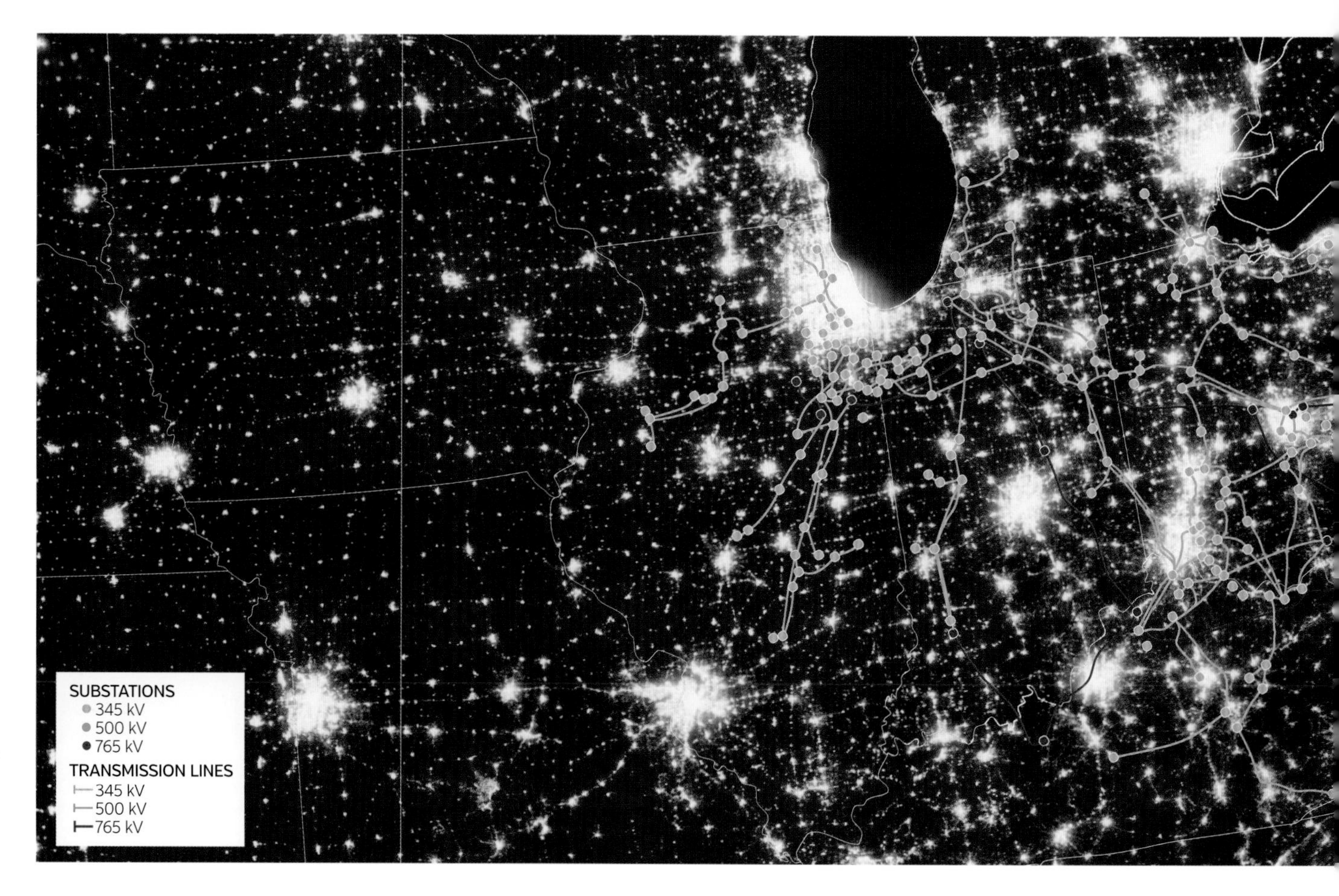

This was, indeed, exactly the approach taken in the 1990s with the establishment of Regional Transmission Operators (RTOs) and Independent System Operators (ISOs) under guidance from the Federal Energy Regulatory Commission. With the goal of ensuring the reliability of the electrical grid, regional and interstate organizations were created to coordinate, control, and monitor the transfer of electricity between states and power companies at much higher voltages than the typical distribution grids of a local utility.

The above map shows what the subenergyshed looks like within the RTO known as "PJM," the world's largest wholesale market for electricity.[13] It resembles the way a basin commission recovers the boundaries of a watershed and internalizes costs and benefits in ways that plausibly increase efficiency and equity in water services in that watershed. PJM supports the reliable and efficient transfer of energy between places by connecting and coordinating the infrastructure that balances load and capacity to optimize the vaue of energy services. It demonstrates the spatial organization of an aspect of the energy system that facilitates the rational management of the value of energy services: the need to interconnect smaller systems to support electric grid reliability. Thus, RTO/ISOs represent a system of subenergysheds in North America.

We refer to PJM as an RTO subenergyshed because of an important difference between watersheds and energysheds. The former is always about water while the energy being transferred in the energyshed can and does take many forms: various combustible fuels, wind, water, solar radiation, thermal sources, nuclear fission, hydrogen, and so on. Each of these energy sources uses different physical and administrative infrastructures to facilitate their transfer to become valuable energy services. These distinct infrastructures have very different regulatory mechanisms and market structures. Natural gas pipelines, electrical grids, gasoline refineries, rooftop solar, and oil being moved by rail freight are transferring energy in distinct energysheds that overlap and interact in complex ways.

These subsystems represent a more complex network structure than subwatersheds. Whereas subwatersheds nest into a relatively simple hierarchy constituting the watershed, these subenergysheds build a web of overlapping and interacting subsystems. It is an empirical question whether, and under what conditions, these various subenergysheds ultimately define a comprehensive regional energyshed with a clearly defined boundary that organizes a critical mass of its parts. However, in regions where inclusive, regional-scale energysheds are

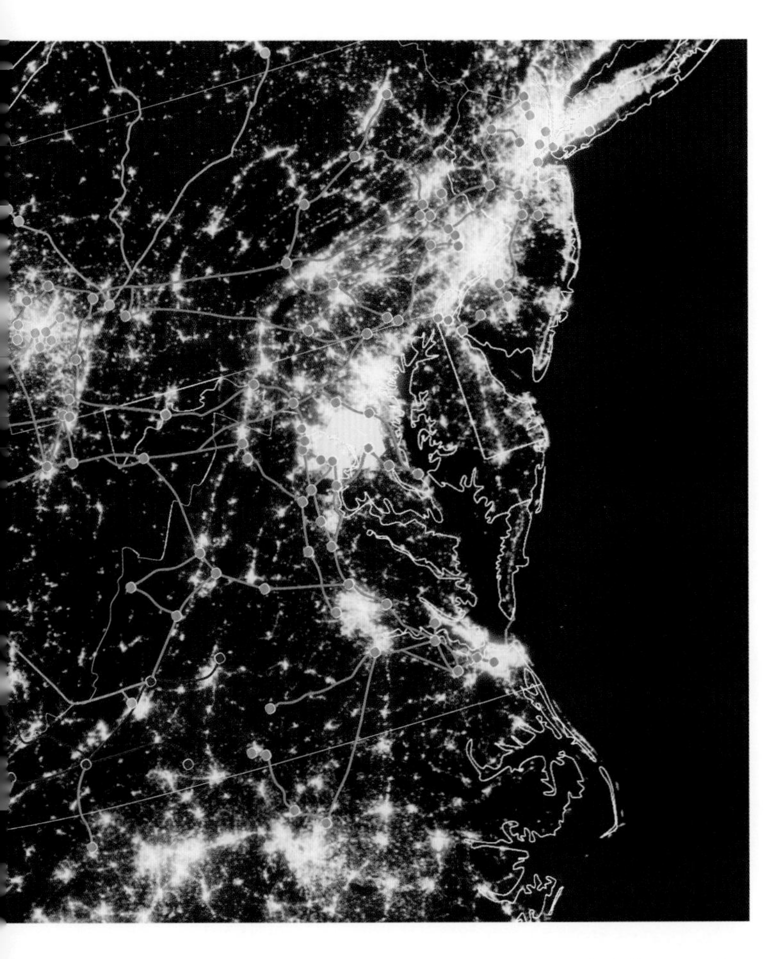

manageable, they have the potential to significantly influence the way energy is generated, transported, and consumed. In a previous essay, we explored the overlapping subenergysheds in the Greater Philadelphia area, and our conclusions strongly suggest that South East Pennsylvania and the tri-state region is a place where the management and governance of an energyshed is achievable.[14] As with the management of watersheds, every region is different and the establishment of a cooperative governance system must come from local and regional efforts. With the success of watershed commissions as a guiding example, utility providers, city governments, private and non-profit organizations should come together to define the boundaries of regional subenergysheds and determine what steps can be taken to unify the management of energy in these regions. Identifying these overlapping boundaries of physical infrastructures and the degree of alignment in the jurisdictions that govern them is a research agenda that we are pursuing at the Kleinman Center. We are confident that this research will yield important policy and design recommendations.

1 International Energy Agency, "World Energy Outlook 2016: Executive Summary" (2016), 4.

2 Ibid., 3.

3 Sustainable Innovation Forum 2015, http://www.cop21paris.org (accessed December 1, 2016).

4 For further details of the features of an energyshed, see Mark Alan Hughes, "Working Paper: The Philadelphia Energyshed," Kleinman Center for Energy Policy (2009), http://www.kleinmanenergy.upenn.edu/paper/working-paper-philadelphia-energyshed (accessed December 1, 2016).

5 Gerald J. Kauffman, "What if...the United States of America Were Based on Watersheds?," *Water Policy* 4 (2002): 57–68.

6 New York State Department of Environmental Conservation, "Delaware River Watershed," http://www.dec.ny.gov/lands/48372.html (accessed December 1, 2016).

7 Delaware River Basin Commission, "Delaware River Basin Compact," http://www.nj.gov/drbc/library/documents/compact.pdf (accessed August 31, 2016).

8 Ibid.

9 Fish and Wildlife Service, "Digest of Federal Resource Laws of Interest to the US Fish and Wildlife Service," https://www.fws.gov/laws/lawsdigest/compact.html (accessed December 1, 2016).

10 Electric Power Research institute, *Electricity Sector Framwork for the Future: Volume 1: Achieving the 21st Century Transformation* (2003) 53.

11 David R. Johnston & Kim Master, *Green Remodeling: Changing the World One Room at a Time* (Gabriola Island, BC Canada: New Society Publishers, 2004), 84.

12 US Energy Information Administration, "Energy Explained: Your Guide to Understanding Energy," http://www.eia.gov/energyexplained/ (accessed December 1, 2016).

13 PJM, "PJM Markets" https://www.pjm.com/~/media/about-pjm/newsroom/fact-sheets/pjms-markets-fact-sheet.ashx (accessed, December 1, 2016).

14 Mark Alan Hughes, "Working Paper: The Philadelphia Energyshed," Kleinman Center for Energy Policy (2009), http://www.kleinmanenergy.upenn.edu/paper/working-paper-philadelphia-energyshed (accessed December 1, 2016).

Left: PJM's backbone transmission system.

ALLISON LASSITER

FLUXES OF RISK

MEASUREMENT AND RESPONSE IN LANDSCAPE INFRASTRUCTURES

Allison Lassiter is an Assistant Professor in City and Regional Planning at the University of Pennsylvania. Her research examines urban water management, including methods of increasing security and resilience to risks associated with climate change. She holds a PhD in Environmental Planning from UC Berkeley and a Masters in City Planning from MIT. Prior to joining Penn, she was a research fellow at Monash University in Melbourne, Australia, working with the Cooperative Research Centre for Water Sensitive Cities.

+ TECHNOLOGY, DESIGN, ENVIRONMENTAL SCIENCE

Opposite: Air pollution over northern China, 2016.
Aerosol Optical Depth:
0 2

Risk is contextual and dynamic: it changes as environmental conditions vary, as assets shift location and worth, and as perceived vulnerabilities fortify or weaken. While landscape and landscape infrastructure have the ability to accommodate and adapt to risk, there are boundaries to responsiveness. At times, environmental stressors are too large, or change too quickly. Can we grow the intelligence of landscapes, allowing them to respond more broadly, rapidly, and reliably to a wider variety of risk variables?

Opportunities to explicitly respond to risk within landscape infrastructure may be rising as the digital technologies of the smart city become increasingly pervasive. Ubiquitous and embedded computing promises to "make a city knowable and controllable in new, more fine-grained, dynamic, and interconnected ways."[1] New landscapes of ecology complemented by electronics, digital technologies, and databases, may allow for maximally robust landscape infrastructure. This essay discusses methods of collecting and responding to data that relate to risk, moving toward a responsive landscape. It concludes by offering critiques of digitally enabled landscape design.

Measuring Risk

Because risk continually changes, measuring risk requires evaluation and reevaluation – an ongoing calculation of the relationships among the environment, its uses, and users. This calls on, as Christophe Girot writes, "a new form of thinking that can integrate the travelling continuum of space and time, rather than present a series of immutable frames in our understanding of landscape."[2] One method of developing this continuum is through granular data streams that capture spatiotemporal risk factors. High-resolution data can be used to identify small departures from the mean in order to find local risks.

BEIJING

Many of the variables associated with environmental risk are already monitored. Government satellites record thermal imagery and take samples of particulate matter in the air. Planes capture topography and surficial changes. Many different types of climate stations–both on land and at sea–record temperature, relative humidity, and precipitation. Formal environmental data collection is proliferating in the city and beyond, increasing in resolution as technology improves and data storage becomes cheaper.

Complementing formal monitoring is a growing number of hyperlocal, ad hoc sensing networks. This do-it-yourself sensing is made possible by the recent proliferation of affordable digital and interactive prototyping platforms. One of the most pervasive development environments is Arduino, an open-source printed circuit board and microcontroller with an accessible coding interface. Arduino and similar platforms (such as Raspberry Pi or BeagleBone) allow the user to set up sensors, collect data, and automate responses based on incoming data streams. There are sensors that measure temperature, the presence of water, motion, magnetism, and electric activity. With platforms like Arduino, it is possible for anyone to engage with sensors, opening the door to a wider variety of people identifying potential risks and measuring relevant, design-scale data.

Automating Response

While sensors are commonly used for ongoing monitoring by scientists and engineers, there are far fewer examples of sensors directly feeding into landscape design programs. Following are some examples of existing responsive design at three scales: plants, ecosystems, and urban landscapes. All are germane to landscape infrastructure, relevant to different types of risk, and necessary to dynamically respond to risk across scale.

Plants

Sensor-responsive environmental design is most common in consumer-facing agriculture and garden products. With a soil moisture sensor, Botanicalls sends a tweet to the owner of a houseplant when the plant needs water. Widely available home irrigation systems customize pre-programmed watering plans based on soil moisture data. A Berlin-based company called INFARM maximizes conditions for intensive urban agriculture installations by reading a suite of sensors, and then manipulates variables like light exposure and microclimate to maximize plant productivity.

For many landscape infrastructure components–including green roofs, green walls, bioswales, rain gardens, urban forests, and constructed wetlands–plant health is critical to the performance of the infrastructure. However, as of yet, there is not the same movement toward responsive interaction in landscape infrastructures. Instead, it is more common to use sensors to analyze past performance. For example, while the New York City Department of Environmental Protection has installed sensors around several new bioswales to measure local precipitation, stormwater infiltration rates, and water quality at inflow and outflow points,[3] there is not currently a program for continuous monitoring or response.

Ecosystems

Operating at a far coarser scale, there is a set of infrastructures at the urban periphery that use fairly small engineered gestures to guide larger ecosystem processes. In the Suisan Marsh in California, a series of gates are opened and closed by operators based on salinity levels of neighboring waters. The gates ensure estuarine tidal flats do not become too salty for native species even as upstream freshwater is drawn off for the state's drinking-water supplies. At these gates, the link between salinity sensing and response is not automated and is not precisely responsive–there are people that intervene in the interpretation of the environmental data and then direct the movement of the salinity gates–yet, there is possibility in dynamically controlling these salinity levels, along with many other types of solute and nutrient flows.

Speculative responsive infrastructure research does just that. A recent project by Brad Cantrell, Justine Holzman, and David Merlin focuses on the sediments that naturally collect behind dams along the Mississippi River.[4] They proposed a new dam construction with multiple outflow doors that open and close in choreographed movements, strategically directing downstream sediment accumulation. The response is informed by several data streams, including real-time topographic sensing. As the sediments deposit, the topographic data indicates which doors should next open and close, ensuring the sediment accumulation meets the intended effect (e.g., habitat creation or earthen levee reinforcement). The intended result is a dynamically sculpted landscape that suits emerging environmental needs.

Urban Landscapes

Between plants and ecosystems are mid-scale, urban landscape infrastructures. In a course I teach, "Landscape Hacking: Environmental Sensing and Responsive Design," students attempt to source and register their own environmental change data. Students learn how to read and write basic Arduino code (C/C++) and how to safely wire circuit boards, including fundamentals of voltage, current, and resistance. Landscape architecture students Elaine Laguerta, Grant Saita, Joe Burg, and Kyle O'Konis, for example, sought to make air pollutants near transit infrastructure visible. They proposed a series of two-meter-tall poles with embedded LED lights that illuminate to indicate levels of local air pollutants. A collection of these poles is scattered across a vacant lot that abuts a highway, revealing a living topography of real-time air quality risk.

Using Arduino as a prototyping environment, their design brought together data from two sensors. The first was a simple gas sensor, which detects the presence of ammonia,

benzene, alcohol, mono-nitrogen oxides, carbon dioxide, and smoke. The students wrote a program for their Arduino that asked the gas sensor to sample the surrounding air every 0.5 seconds. Based on the primary gas detected at that moment, they programmed the lights in the pole to change color along an RGB spectrum. All the lights in the pole were lit the same color, corresponding with the sensed pollutant.

The second sensor was a simple, thermal wind sensor that detected wind speed. The students assumed that wind in the area would dissipate pollutant loads (this assumption could be tested with different sensors able to explicitly measure gas concentrations; however, such sensors were unavailable to the students during the course). They programmed the light pole to show a visible reduction in pollutant load by decreasing the height of the activated lights on the pole proportionate to the sensed wind speed. The lights were at maximum height when there was no wind and dropped in height as the wind increased. The height of the lights updated every 0.5 seconds.

The students built a prototype pole that they demonstrated within the studio. Though visually compelling, the design was constrained by the limits of both the Arduino platform and the sensors. The sensors were chosen because they were inexpensive, easy to use, and reasonably durable; however, neither sensor was sufficiently sensitive to detect small variations. In particular, the gas sensor was not able to detect low concentrations of pollutants and therefore was unable to capture the expected variation of pollutant concentrations observed at the vacant lot site. Their design remains challenging to scale into a long-term, outdoor installation. While Arduino is useful for ideation and prototyping, the hardware is not intended for outdoor weather conditions or continuous, prolonged use. Durable, higher voltage systems are certainly possible, but most likely require moving away from Arduino into more advanced circuitry and an associated electrical infrastructure.

Risk-Responsive Landscape Infrastructures

Digitally enabled design has the potential to increase the resilience and adaptive capacity of landscape infrastructure by engaging the best of both landscape design

Above: Ebb and Flow, a vertical farm installation by INFARM.

and smart city technologies. Yet, there are many barriers to implementation. Beyond technological constraints, the most significant challenges are in the ability to react to data streams in real time and the meaningfulness of automated solutions. Common to almost all digital infrastructure proposals is the concern that sensing and response technologies may not be robust over time. In addition to broken wires and connections, hardware can quickly become obsolete. Obsolescence is a problem with all infrastructures—even landscape infrastructure—but one of the pervasive arguments for landscape solutions is that landscape can be low cost and resilient over the long term. The risk then is that integration with digital and electronic technologies could render landscapes "buggy and brittle."[5]

Even if reliable, determining when and how to respond to sensor data is far more difficult than collecting it. Defining the transitions—that is, deciding when to program the system to change from one automated output to the next—is problematic for all but the simplest systems. A risk-responsive infrastructure would require many assumptions and reductions. One of the most fundamental is that it is necessary to classify thresholds of risk in order to link sensed data to responses. The thresholds will almost always be broadly defined as follows: (1) movement in the measured data captures noise, or expected variability in the system; (2) the data reveal a departure from historic relationships, ranging from tolerable change to increasing stages of risk; (3) the magnitude or rate of change in the data indicates immediate and extreme risk, approaching failure. Exactly when, especially in a multivariate system, does sensor data indicate different stages of risk? In some cases, defining the risks may be reasonably clear—for example, where a specific salinity level is known to kill a key plant species—but determining the most appropriate automated response is always far fuzzier.

Managing the climate surrounding a plant, directing the solutes dissolved in a stream of water, or visualizing pollutants are all relatively straightforward. Each example has a set of input variables that is easy to measure and can be reasonably linked to discrete responses. Notably, each sidesteps integrating with human systems, which are less predictable and challenging to measure and encode. In the case of the Mississippi River sediment sculpting project, the environmental management outcome (earthen levee reinforcement) is predetermined. In actuality, it can take years of negotiations with stakeholders to agree on environmental interventions - this is likely the most intractable part of the sediment management problem. Though the project may be able to adaptively optimize sediment deposition, it is unlikely it could fluidly move from one outcome to another without a substantial degree of human intervention.

Lastly, there are significant challenges in linking scales of sensing and response: sensed data may reveal a risk symptomatic of a problem whose cause is distant in time or space. Do we treat the symptom, the cause, or both? In some cases, managing the local effects of a distant risk is necessary. In other cases, it may be Sisyphean, indicating that hyperlocal monitoring must feed into a broader or deeper problem-solving strategy.

Responsive systems are likely best suited to solving simple problems. Sensor technologies, defining thresholds, and the judgments embedded in linking risks to responses are all reductive. Reduction and simplification are necessary for all measured and modeled systems. These pathologies may not be compatible with many complex systems, including those deeply integrated with social processes. Many of the largest

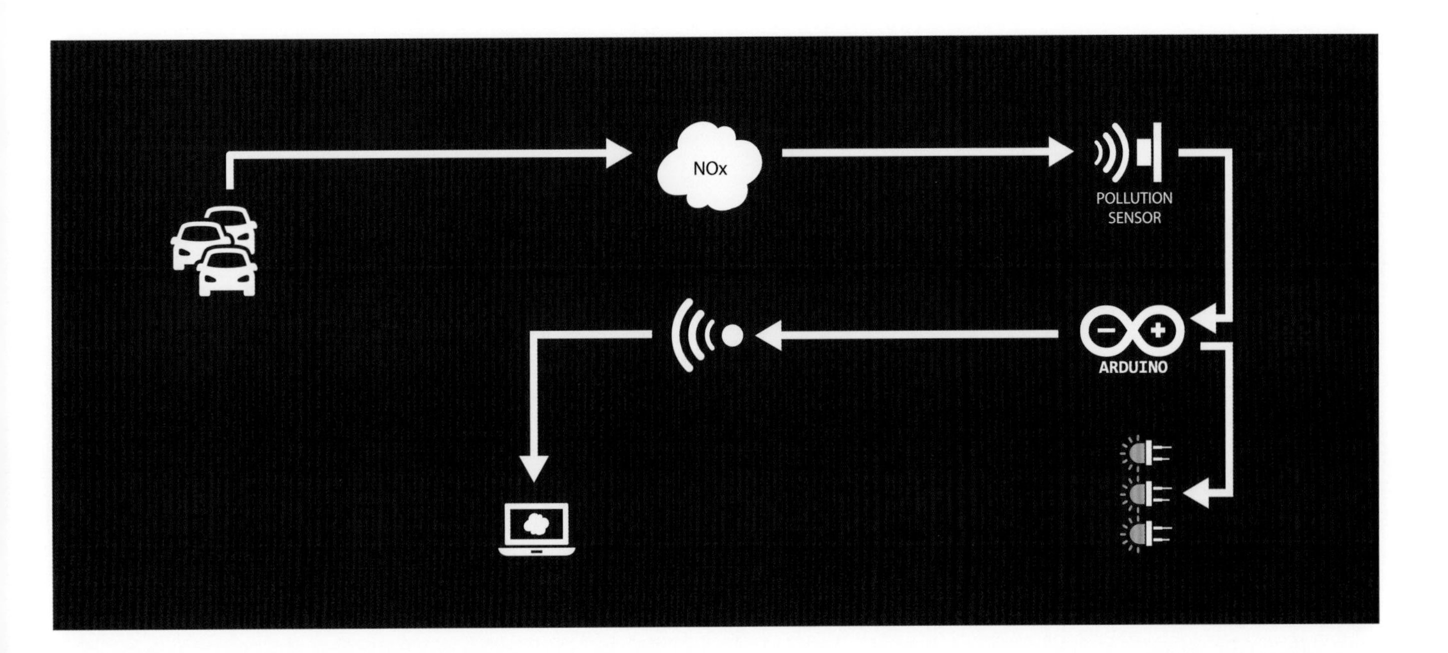

risks that landscape infrastructure grapples with are beyond the limits of automation. Nonetheless, blurring the boundary between landscape and digital solutions creates a stronger suite of urban infrastructures – a portfolio that varies from low technology green to traditionally engineered, with many gradations in between. Further, many complex problems can be broken down into a series of smaller, compounding risks, some of which may be reasonably handled through responsive landscape design. A maximally robust infrastructure, able to accommodate risk as it fluxes over space and time, will rely on both landscape *and* emerging, digital technologies.

1 Rob Kitchin, "The Real-time City? Big Data and Smart Urbanism," *GeoJournal* 79, no. 1 (2014): 1–14.

2 Christophe Girot, "Vision in Motion," in Charles Waldheim (ed.), *The Landscape Urbanism Reader* (San Francisco: Chronicle Books, 2006), 96.

3 James McLaughlin, "NYC Bioswales Pilot Project Improves Stormwater Management," https://nywea.org/clearwaters/12-2-summer/7.pdf (accessed July 24, 2016).

4 Bradley Cantrell and Justine Holzman, "Synthetic Ecologies: protocols, simulation, and manipulation for indeterminate landscapes," *Proceedings of the 34th Annual Conference of the Association for Computer Aided Design in Architecture* (Los Angeles, 2014), 709–18.

5 Anthony Townsend suggests the smart city may be "buggy, brittle, and bugged" in *Smart Cities: Big Data, Civic Hackers, and the Quest for a New Utopia* (New York: W.W. Norton & Company, 2013), 253.

Left: Rendering of pollution sensor poles.
Above: Sensor input and output diagram.

MATTHEW WALTNER-TOEWS + DAVID WALTNER-TOEWS

DESIGNED FOR DISEASE?

AN ECOYSTEM APPROACH TO EMERGING INFECTIOUS DISEASE

In 1967, US surgeon-general William Stewart declared that "because [they] have been largely controlled in the United States, we can now close the book on infectious diseases."[1] By 1995, however, the director of the Centers for Disease Control and Prevention spoke of "recent disquieting infectious disease trends" and the "fragile equilibrium between humans and infectious microorganisms."[2] Emerging infectious diseases (EIDs) were defined as new infections in a population, or existing infections that were spreading rapidly within populations or across landscapes. In the decades since then, interest and alarm exploded in equal proportion, with new EIDs being identified almost daily. These included AIDS, Avian Influenza, Lyme Disease, New-Variant Creuzfeldt-Jakob Disease (Mad Cow Disease), SARS, foodborne infections such as those caused by *E.coli*, and diseases caused by a variety of drug-resistant bacteria, as well as the West Nile, Nipah, Zika, and Ebola viruses.[3]

More than 60% of EIDs come from animals, with those originating from food animals and wildlife being of greatest concern. The main drivers of this disease emergence have been socio-economic and environmental, including human demographics and behavior, economic development, land use, international travel and commerce, microbial adaptation, climate change, and breakdown of public health measures.[4] Our responses to EIDs have included development of drugs and vaccines, and "genomics-associated advances in microbial detection and treatment, improved disease surveillance, and greater awareness of EIDs and the complicated variables that underlie emergence."[5] The larger environmental and social issues are acknowledged but rarely addressed.

In part, these social and environmental issues have not been tackled because they have been considered to be outside the mandate of health systems. These mandates, in turn, are embedded in a self-serving understanding of sciences that decontextualizes events and organisms, and is driven by linear narratives that privilege economically and politically powerful interest groups.[7] The idea that diseases emerged from the dynamic relationships between people and places was not (until the advent of GIS) considered to be serious, quantitative science, and was relegated to popular books on natural history.

There are reasons beyond political and economic biases, however, that make addressing the fundamental drivers of infectious diseases problematic. Many EIDs are the unintended consequences of responses to health and environmental concerns of previous generations. Economies of scale, international trade, and monocultures in agriculture have enabled many parts of the world to achieve Henry IV's dream of "a chicken in every pot," but are also associated with the global spread of foodborne diseases, as well as agri-food-system-associated diseases such as avian influenza and SARS. Urban stormwater, sewage, and water treatment systems–designed and built in response to recurrent epidemics of cholera and typhoid fever in the 19th century–up-scaled household hygiene problems to cities and regions. Systems designed in Europe and North America at these larger geographic scales rely on increasingly unrealistic stable weather patterns, water flows, and investments in infrastructure. Restructuring of the agri-food and urban water systems are themselves embedded in complex webs of stunning population increases and rapid urbanization over the past century (which further reflect the successes of previous interventions) and infrastructure is often 'improved' by building over older versions of similar systems.

Matthew Waltner-Toews holds a Masters of Landscape Architecture from the University of Guelph, Canada, where he completed a thesis on urban landscape design and management implications for the reduction of West Nile Virus. After a few years of landscape architectural practice, he is now raising bees in Australia.

David Waltner-Toews, is an epidemiologist specializing in zoonotic diseases and a Professor Emeritus at the University of Guelph, Canada. He is author of a number of books on emerging diseases including *The Chickens Fight Back: Pandemic Panics and Deadly Diseases That Jump from Animals to Humans* (2009) and *The Origin of Feces: What Excrement Tells Us About Evolution, Ecology, and a Sustainable Society* (2013).

+ EPIDEMIOLOGY, PLANNING, ENTOMOLOGY

What kind of strategy might enable landscape architects and public health workers to navigate this complex terrain and design reasonable responses? The "ecosystem approach" was developed as an approach to environmental management and sustainability based on ecological thinking and research. Initially articulated by the scientific advisory committee of the International Joint Commission of the Great Lakes Basin, the approach has diversified over time such that it has now come to be applied not only to the study and achievement of outcomes related to biodiversity and species conservation, but also to the health and well-being of selected species, including people. Rooted in a complex systems understanding of the world–where social and ecological variables interact in uncertain and unexpected ways–this approach offers a useful way to think about EIDs and how one might prevent them.[8]

The ecosystem approach entails an integration of systems thinking with public involvement, bringing together interested people from the community with a wide range of experts and professionals. This changes the nature, and evaluation, of allowable evidence, and tends to shift the focus away from what is seen as pure science to something more akin to professional practice. The goal is to achieve sustainable health outcomes through more adept managing of human-environmental interactions.[9] In practice, ecosystem approaches to health are grounded in participation by stakeholders living in defined landscapes and ecosystems. This being the case, who speaks for the ecosystems, or the land? Who speaks for the diversity of non-human species that live around us? And if future outbreaks are embedded in complex interactions among ecosystems, non-human species, and people, we might ask: who speaks for how we might design a convivial landscape for future generations?

In thinking about this, the relationship between the introduction, explosive spread, and subsequent persistence of West Nile Virus (WNV) in North America suggests some late lessons that could inform future actions.[10] WNV was first isolated and identified, in 1937, from a febrile woman in Uganda, but has since been shown to have been endemic, probably for millennia, in birds and other animals along a flyway between Africa, the Near East, and Europe. Until the mid-1990s, infection with the virus in these areas was only rarely associated with serious neurological disease. Then, in the hot summer of 1999, investigators from the Center for Disease Control (CDC) were notified of an outbreak of neurological disease in New York City. Suggestions by a veterinarian at the Bronx Zoo that high mortality in crows in the same area might be related were dismissed by CDC officials. Animals–and certainly crows–were outside their mandate, and crow-deaths did not fit with the official medical story of what was happening.

Beginning that year and in the years that followed, WNV disease (as it was belatedly recognized to be) spread across North America in seasonal waves. A decade later, tens of thousands of cases and about a thousand deaths had been reported across Canada and the United States. Among the many questions raised by the explosive spread of this epidemic are those related to North American landscapes: was there something about the way we had designed our urban areas that facilitated spread of the disease?

West Nile and similar viruses such as the St. Louis, Western, and Eastern Equine encephalitis viruses, are transmitted from certain species of infected passerine birds (such as robins and grackles, which serve as virus amplifiers) to some species of mosquitoes, and then to mammals, such as horses and people. Not all bird species are amplifiers: corvids, such as crows and jays, suffer high mortality and, while serving as early warning that the virus is circulating, are not important in its amplification and spread. Neither horses nor people appear to develop a sufficiently high viremia to reinfect mosquitoes. From a landscape design point of view, then, habitat for the relevant mosquitoes and birds invite closer examination.

Over 20 mosquito species have been implicated in the spread of WNV in North America, but the mosquitoes that are of most concern have been *Culex pipiens* in the east and *Culex tarsalis* in the west. Both are active at dusk and dawn, spend most of their time in the tree canopy, and feed mostly on birds. Towards the end of the summer season, however, both species shift host preference and start to feed on mammals as well

as birds. Both are well adapted to urban environments. *Culex pipiens* prefers water that is high in organics, and is possibly the most pollution-tolerant of all mosquitoes, being frequently found in sewage treatment plant effluent. *Culex tarsalis* seeks out water with decomposing vegetation (roadside ditches, for instance), and have been known to develop the first batch of eggs without a blood meal in as little as four days after emergence. Both mosquito species are opportunistic container breeders, and will lay eggs in nearly any standing water. Both species overwinter as adults, and seek out humid, sheltered places for this purpose.

How do these ecological variables relate to landscape design? Storm sewers, which carry water runoff from residential and commercial properties, are often situated under concrete roadways. The sewers are warmed from above by the streets; this warming represents a localized example of the more general 'heat island' phenomenon, in which concrete absorbs and re-radiates heat. The heat island effect means that the downtown areas of cities are generally warmer than surrounding green spaces. Being semi-stagnant and underground, storm sewers are also free of insect predators such as fish. All these characteristics make storm sewers an ideal habitat for breeding, and overwintering, of certain species of mosquito.[11] Furthermore, many urban and sub-urban landscapes that provide important living space and fresh air for people, also offer excellent habitat for the bird species, such as sparrows, finches, and grackles, which are most competent hosts for WNV.

A few studies by ecologists have concluded that populations of plants, mammals, birds, and insects living in ecosystems with low biodiversity tend to be more adversely affected by host-specific disease, and more effective at spreading it, than populations in ecosystems with high biodiversity. Because potential host populations in these low-diversity areas are less constrained by competing species and predators, the hosts tend to be more densely distributed, and more likely to spread disease among themselves. This "dilution effect" of high biodiversity ecosystems appears to hold true for Lyme disease transmission in the United States;[12] is it also true for WNV?

In Sweden, researchers found a direct relationship between the amount of biodiverse green space (forest and preserved natural ecosystems) and bird populations in urban areas.[13] Species diversity for woodpeckers, hole nesters, and forest birds increased from the city center to the periphery, along with vegetation diversity. However, urban birds were concentrated in the residential area. While the residential habitat supported large numbers of birds, the species diversity was quite low, suggesting that while the habitat was good for specific urban birds, it was hostile or unsuitable for many other species. The researchers suggested that the green wedge of the greenway increased species richness for nearby areas, and they concluded from the data that increasing the number of greenways into the city should increase the species diversity for the entire

Above Left: Genetic code of Zika virus.

area, including the city center. Vegetative groundcover was also positively correlated with species richness.

The Swedish study of avian biodiversity in cities is especially pertinent to WNV. All of the 10 most WNV virally-competent birds in the United States and Canada could be qualified as "urban birds," based on their prevalence in annual backyard bird counts.[14] Jays, robins, and grackles are common backyard birds across North America, while crows and magpies are common urban scavengers. Both finches and sparrows are also ubiquitous in urban areas. While many of these birds migrate in the wild, many urban birds stay all winter, because their food sources (backyard bird feeders, roadkill, and dumpsters, to name a few) remain.

Urban birds, such as those mentioned above, are successful in cities and neighborhoods because they can use urban environments better than other birds, based on their dietary and nesting requirements. What ties many of these birds together is their need for clear ground to forage on and large trees for nesting or roosting. The mature tree canopies and open lawns found in many residential environments, when taken together with stagnant storm sewers and concrete-generated heat islands, create a high-risk environment for the maintenance and spread of WNV as well as other, similar, viruses.[15]

If we take an ecosystem approach, bringing together residents, planners, ecologists, disease ecologists, and health specialists, what sorts of strategies for risk minimization might we propose? In the first instance, we should be clear that the relevant ecological variables will vary from place to place, depending on temperature, rainfall, species present, and so on. Furthermore, many of the variables interact with each other, so that there is unlikely to be any single intervention that by itself will result in more disease-resistant communities.[16] Having said that, we can make a few generalizations for temperate areas of North America.

1) Reduce or remove mosquito habitat. This will mean different things in different climates, but in general it means increasing infiltration as much as possible, and reuse of runoff water. In some climates this might mean rain gardens, and in others rock gardens. If storm water is not going into subsurface stagnant holding tanks or pipes, and is being reused and infiltrated into the soil, then mosquitoes cannot use it as habitat. Many existing studies and neighborhoods around the world already apply these concepts. Where infiltration is not possible, standing water needs to be capable of supporting mosquito predators.

2) Reduce heat island effect. Again, this can mean different things for different climates. Narrower streets with porous paving or low-albedo paving material would be effective in many places. 'Green roofs' on houses would also help in this regard.

3) Redesign greenspace. Not all greenspace is equal. Lawn decreases the heat island effect, improves water infiltration, and is good for a soccer pitch. However, lawns can also increase WNV risk through providing bird and mosquito habitat. Planting native vegetation and attempting to create a complex, biodiverse urban ecosystem would likely reduce mosquito-borne risk by encouraging more mosquito predators.

4) Consider subsurface drainage as an issue of disease ecology. Subsurface drainage is an important part of many urban designs. Designers should consider the appropriate slope required for effective drainage, fewer catch basins (or basins that promote mosquito predators), innovations in pipe design (such as to allow for intentional leakage in places where water would otherwise collect), and reduction in water runoff (via maximization of water infiltration on sites). Municipally owned and maintained sewage systems and land drainage systems are standard in North American city design. They do not have to introduce or increase disease risk.

Part of the challenge in implementing these kinds of changes is that many of them require fundamental, and costly, shifts in urban culture, landscape aesthetics, and design, with no certainty of desirable outcomes. A more open communication and collaboration between those knowledgeable and passionate about biological diversity, landscape design, and health would at least provide a basis for how one might formulate the appropriate questions and assess the effects of change over time. By bringing together and engaging planners, scientists, and the general public, we can begin to reimagine and redesign our landscapes in ways that are ecologically grounded and socially acceptable, going beyond merely minimizing WNV disease risks, to nurturing resilient and healthy communities.

1 Ross Upshur, "Ethics and Infectious Disease," *Bulletin of the World Health Organization* 86, no. 8 (2008).

2 David Satcher, "Emerging Infections: Getting Ahead of the Curve," *Emerging Infectious Diseases* 1, no. 1 (1995).

3 Kate E. Jones et al., "Global Trends in Emerging Infectious Diseases" *Nature* (2008) 990–93.

4 Joshua Lederberg, Robert Shope & Stanley Oaks (eds), *Emerging Infections: Microbial Threats to Health in the United States* (Washington, DC: National Academy Press, 1992).

5 David M. Morens & Anthony S. Fauci, "Emerging Infectious Diseases in 2012: 20 Years after the Institute of Medicine Report," *mBio* 3 no. 6 (2012): e00494-12.

6 Kevin Bardosh (ed.), *One Health: Science, Politics and Zoonotic Disease in Africa* (London: Earthscan, 2016).

7 Tim H.F. Allen, B.L. Bandursky & A.W. King, *The Ecosystem Approach: Theory and Ecosystem Integrity: A Report to the International Joint Commission of the Great Lakes* (1993).

8 David Waltner-Toews, James J. Kay & Nina-Marie Lister (eds), *The Ecosystem Approach: Complexity, Uncertainty, and Managing for Sustainability* (New York: Columbia University Press, 2008).

9 Dominique Charron (ed.), *Ecohealth Research in Practice: Innovative Applications of an Ecosystem Approach to Health* (Ottawa: Springer, 2012).

10 Although the 21st-century agri-food system is associated with the emergence and spread of a variety of serious emerging diseases, the geographic disconnect between urban consumers and rural landscapes, the economics and politics of global trade, and the complexities of multiple, conflicting, stakeholder goals at multiple scales, make agriculture and food a thornier and less tractable case from a realistic design perspective: see Jones, et al., "Global Trends in Emerging Infectious Diseases."

11 K. Byrne & R.A. Nichols "*Culex pipiens* in London underground tunnels: differentiation between surface and subterranean populations," *Heredity* 82 (1999): 7–15.

12 Richard Ostfeld & Felicia Keesing, "Biodiversity and Disease Risk: The Case of Lyme Disease," *Conservation Biology* 14, no. 3 (2000): 722–28.

13 U.G. Sandström, P. Angelstam & G. Mikusinski, "Ecological Diversity of Birds in Relation to the Structure of Urban Green Space," *Landscape and Urban Planning* 77 (2006): 39–53.

14 Cornell Lab of Ornithology and The Audubon Society, "The Great Backyard Bird Count 2007," http://www.birdsource.org/gbbc/ (accessed September 7, 2016).

15 Matthew Waltner-Toews, "Urban Landscape Design and Management Implications for Reducing West Nile Virus," Master of Landscape Architecture Thesis, University of Guelph (2008).

16 S.E. Bowden, K. Magori & J.M. Drake, "Regional differences in the association between land cover and West Nile virus disease incidence in humans in the United States," *American Journal of Tropical Medicine and Hygiene* 84, no. 2 (2011): 234–38.

WHAT DOESN'T KILL YOU

Thomas Oles is Professor of Landscape Architecture and Design Theory at the Swedish University of Agricultural Sciences. He is the author of *Go With Me: 50 Steps to Landscape Thinking* (2013) and *Walls: Enclosure and Ethics in the Modern Landscape* (2014).

Phoebe Lickwar is Principal of Forge Landscape Architecture and Assistant Professor of Landscape Architecture at the University of Arkansas. She holds degrees in landscape architecture, art history, and education from Rhode Island School of Design and Harvard University. In 2016, she was selected as landscape architect on the winning multi-disciplinary team for the National WWI Memorial.

+ EDUCATION

THOMAS OLES + PHOEBE LICKWAR

We write as landscape architecture educators. We teach in different institutions–different countries, in fact–and our students come to us from dramatically different backgrounds. We do not pledge allegiance to any particular school or creed, and our interests and tastes often diverge. We have no common 'agenda' as such.

But we do have a common concern. Year after year, studio after studio, we have noticed more and more timidity among our students. We have witnessed growing reluctance to pursue marginal or fantastic ideas, to experiment with different or weird modes of expression, to confront messy or insoluble questions. Indeed, we have noticed increasing avoidance of messiness altogether, our students' desks looking more like those of Jack Lemmon and his faceless coworkers in *The Apartment* than the sites of wreckage–coagulated glue, discarded trace, old coffee cups–we remember from our own education. We have noticed a locking down, a fear of exposure, an almost obsessive avoidance of even the appearance of ignorance, or weakness, or awe.

In short, we have witnessed growing aversion to *risk* in all its forms.

But what, exactly, do we mean by risk? Etymology can tell us something. The modern word risk, meaning "exposure to the possibility of loss, injury, or other adverse or unwelcome circumstance," derives from the Latin *resicum* and Greek *risikon*, words that originally denoted damage incurred in the maritime transport of goods. The deeper origins of the Latin and Greek words are contested. Some propose that risk derived from a now-lost Latin noun denoting 'something that cuts' (a crag, a rock that wrecks a ship). Others have suggested that their origin lies in the Arabic *rizq*, meaning 'provision' or 'lot,' and hence also 'property' and 'wealth' (a hypothesis supported by the frequent juxtaposition of *resicum* and *fortuna* in Latin). At root, the Arabic word probably referred to any "thing from which a person profits or derives advantage."

Such advantage was invariably fickle in the ancient world. Some were smiled upon by fate while others were punished. The main metaphor of medieval Europe was the wheel of fortune, and the place where one landed on it had little to do with merit or morals or money. Life was a gamble, and the deck was hopelessly stacked. What we now call risk was simply the condition of being alive in the world, woven into the very fabric of existence. One could no more evade it than one could stop eating or breathing.

It was only in the modern era that risk became predictable. Quite suddenly it was possible to know in advance, and with great accuracy, the likelihood that an action or behavior would lead to injury or death. As it turned out, the wheel of fortune was weighted: people fell far more often in some places than in others. This created the conditions under which risk could be converted into a commodity. On one hand, predictable risk led to the development of modern insurance and risk management. On the other, it made possible the marketing of risk as pleasure. "Experienced climbers," writes geographer Yi-Fu Tuan in *Landscapes of Fear*, "abhor danger while welcoming risk."[1] Modern statistics provided the means to know the difference. Bungee jumpers jump and hang gliders glide because they know that self-extinction in the pursuit of their particular thrill is acceptably unlikely. The rush is worth the risk.

And yet, even if risk sells cars and package vacations, biology and culture nevertheless condition us to avoid it. Risky behavior, despite (or because of) its allure, is still widely seen as aberrant. The Diagnostic and Statistical Manual of Mental Disorders, for example, defines "engagement in dangerous, risky, and potentially self-damaging activities" as a pathological personality trait.[2] Why would one deliberately expose oneself to experiences from which the body recoils, creating sensations ranging from vague discomfort to sheer terror? And, even more perplexing, why would one pay money for those experiences? The fact is, whatever its value in the marketplace, we are hard wired to shun risk, not seek it.

Perhaps it is not so strange, then, that we should see an aversion to risk among our students. They are already vulnerable enough, lacking the confidence, skill, and indifference to others' opinions that come with age and experience. It is perfectly reasonable that they would want to reduce their exposure to forces they cannot control, not least the verdicts of peers and teachers that (as anyone who has gone through a design education will attest) can cut deeper than any knife. And when they are finished and emerge with a professional credential, these students are confronted, at least in the United States, by a neoliberal reality in which the reward for taking risks–for one deviant step on the narrow path laid down by landscape architecture programs, accreditation boards, and professional organizations–is the very real prospect of penury and no benefits.

But if risk cuts, surely it cuts both ways. Students who avoid exposure may increase their comfort level, but they severely limit the extent of their own learning. It seems strange to have to write this when not so long ago it would have been self-evident. In the 1960s and 1970s, risk was seen as an inherent value in all education, essential to developing both creativity and competence, and landscape architecture education was no exception. This was paralleled by an atmosphere of experimentation in the profession as a whole, with many practitioners developing and testing methods that departed in radical ways from those of their predecessors. It is no exaggeration to say that the work of these designers and of those who follow in their footsteps–however inscrutable or idiosyncratic–is among the most admired and emulated in the profession today.

Professional programs in landscape architecture often stress creativity and 'innovation,' and the 'transformative' nature of landscape architecture education, in their marketing texts. The aspiration is admirable, but we wonder if this is false advertising. Real creativity–and real learning–is always a risky voyage. It is always uncomfortable and sometimes excruciating. It always means navigating stormy seas without a compass, and it inevitably leaves cuts, scrapes, and scars.

In contrast, more and more of landscape architecture education–and indeed landscape architecture itself–seems to be about risk management rather than risk taking, about control of the world rather than exposure to it. This has noticeably diminished student creativity, in our view. But even if one remains unconvinced by this reasoning, the fact is that limiting student exposure to risk is simply poor preparation for the realities of landscape architecture practice today. At a time of profound uncertainty about the course of human–indeed all–life on earth, it creates a dangerous illusion of control where there is none. Perhaps more than in any other profession, the landscape architect is always 'exposed' to this uncertainty, always vulnerable in the face of too many variables. Forget the near-impossibility of designing landscapes to withstand rising seas and superstorms - there is often no defense even against those *predictable* forces that conspire to transform, undermine, or destroy landscapes. Liability insurance might protect against future negligence claims or disasters, but it is powerless against the virtual certainties of political change, economic crisis, vandalism, and atrophy.

It does landscape architecture students no service to conceal this reality. University faculty (at least those with tenure, a shrinking minority) are some of the most protected people in the modern workplace, partly or wholly insulated from the economic exigencies that professional designers routinely confront, and which await most of their students on graduation. They enjoy freedoms that, however diminished in recent years, are nonetheless entirely exceptional. Avoidance of risk on the part of these educators is thus not only unethical but also incomprehensible.

What would a risky landscape architecture education look like? For one thing, it would dramatically shift focus toward field engagements of every conceivable kind. It would mean engaging sites in ways that are largely avoided today, from deliberate acts of trespass and transgression, to exposing oneself to social situations in which one feels vulnerable or off-balance, to using the body and its senses more fully–and more deliberately–in the production of landscape knowledge. It also suggests a wider array of studio practices, in which deviation from established conventions and norms is rewarded rather than punished. These day-to-day practices would be paralleled by far more vocal critique of capitalism: a system on which landscape architecture depends for its bread but that has now come to threaten more or less everything that truly matters.

Many children now grow up in a world where they never taste water from a stream, never climb a tree, never touch another species. A world where the cities and towns and villages they call home may disappear from the Earth within their lifetimes. Surely, in such a world, the time for politeness is long past. Landscape architecture educators must loudly proclaim that

a different way of knowing the world and being in the world is possible. They must become brave and loud in their embrace of practices that sometimes provoke disdain from their academic peers and superiors. They must become *disobedient* in the sense used by Henry David Thoreau and Hannah Arendt, and be prepared to live with the consequences. They must leave their cozy harbors and venture out onto the rough seas of opprobrium and ridicule.

This will be painful, to be sure. It will change the place of landscape architecture departments in the institutions in which they operate. The risk of damage, or even wreckage, is real. But there is no choice. It is only *out there*–where they and we are vulnerable–that we can teach students the practices that are essential if this profession is to remain one of risk takers rather than risk managers, one that challenges causes rather than merely mitigating effects. Like blood-letters of old, we must cut deep enough to heal but not to kill.

1 Yi-Fu Tuan, *Landscapes of Fear* (New York: Pantheon, 1979), 202.

2 American Psychiatric Association, *Diagnostic and Statistical Manual of Mental Disorders: DSM-5* (Washington, DC: American Psychiatric Association, 2013), 780.

IN CONVERSATION WITH
MATTHIJS BOUW

Matthijs Bouw is the founder of One Architecture [Amsterdam and New York] and the Rockefeller Urban Resilience Fellow at PennDesign. In collaboration with the Bjarke Ingels Group [BIG], Bouw co-led development of the "BIG U" – a sweeping proposal for surge protection around Lower Manhattan developed during the Rebuild by Design competition. The project received $335 million in Community Development Block Grant funding to construct its first phase: the Eastside Coastal Resiliency Project. Billy Fleming caught up with Matthijs in Philadelphia on behalf of LA+ Journal.

+ Can you give us a quick update about where the Big U or Dryline is in the design and approval process?

Sure. Out of the Rebuild by Design [RBD] process came two projects – one of them is a project called the Eastside Coastal Resiliency Project, which is run by the New York City Department of Design and Construction. It is for the area between East 25th Street and Montgomery Street. That project is now in preliminary design with the idea of starting construction [in mid-2018].

That project is driven very much by some harsh funding requirements, as we anticipated when we got into the RBD competition. We realized that if we wanted to win, we needed to design a project that HUD [the US Department of Housing and Urban Development] could work with. We knew how big the project could be financially, we knew that we needed to build everything onshore [to avoid] getting into permitting issues that take a lot of time, and to aim for the right level of integration with private entities and different city entities so that they could digest it. Otherwise, the City of New York would not be able to implement it in time [to meet the requirements of the HUD grant].

The second project is the Lower Manhattan Coastal Resiliency project, where we do the design work, again with BIG, and now AECOM's landscape studio. That project focuses on the area between Montgomery Street down to the Battery and then up north to the northern end of Battery Park City. So, that's another, let's say, three miles, and it's more or less divided into two sections. First is the Two Bridges section, which is between Montgomery Street and the Brooklyn Bridge. That section has been funded through the National Disaster Resiliency Competition [NDRC] and there again we have a short timeline and a HUD-funded budget to work with for implementation.

Then we also have the area from Brooklyn Bridge down to the rest of Battery Park City where the exercise at this stage is still in the planning phase – it's only partially funded. The focus of the exercise now is to try and better understand the dimensions of the projects: what you would do in the near term, and what you would do in the longer term if new funding possibilities opened up. The perspective is not yet driven by finance per se, but more about designing for future funding streams and what can you do in response to them.

+ Can you tell us about some of the specific constraints that you and your colleagues were cognizant of during the competition and how your design decisions responded to them? How did you approach the design process differently as a result of those constraints?

There were two, interrelated big moves that came as a result of what HUD was telling us they could handle. The whole idea of the BIG U as a wrap-around barrier system came from the fact that the City, in the SIRR Report, said that they needed an integrated coastal protection system across the whole of Lower Manhattan. When you looked at all the assets in the floodplain, it was quite clear that, no matter what else we did, we had to respond to that concern. That got us interested in the question of, 'OK, how do you build a big coastal barrier across a densely populated island like Manhattan without disrupting everyone's connection to the waterfront? Or how do you do that while enhancing access to the edge? So, not only how do you keep from undoing all these recent gains that the City made in reconnecting people to the waterfront, but how do you build on that and reduce the risk to all of those people and assets in the surge zone?

One move we made in response to that was to try and create these social infrastructures along the edge that could provide multiple urban benefits - and we knew that you could not deliver on that goal, or really even understand what the possibilities of such a project were, if we didn't work through those questions with the people who live there. So, we decided to scale everything down and break the project up into component parts so that we could have conversations with multiple local constituencies about how to make this massive barrier into an amenity.

The second element that proved important was that, as the competition went on, it became increasingly clear to us that the terms of the competition–what would make you win–were not very clear. But we took a guess and said, OK, there's momentum and there's funding after Sandy, all of which will dissipate. So, for us to be successful and responsive to both HUD's limitations and the need to design something in cooperation with the people living in Lower Manhattan, we proposed something that we knew could be built while that momentum was still behind us, and that, hopefully, could be carried on and improved upon as New York City thought about longer-term adaptation strategies. That meant no offshore [interventions]–whether for wave attenuation or ecological benefit–because the permitting process would never allow you to build something within HUD's timeline. It also meant breaking the BIG U into a bunch of smaller parts because, in this country, you cannot build such a $3 billion infrastructure project. Quite frankly, in the SIRR Report the City had already made it clear that it would be unwise to do a coastal barrier that runs under the Verrazano Bridge because it would take too much time to approve and build. That allowed us to look at what was available. We thought if there was $1 billion set aside for RBD, maybe $400 million would go to New York City and that meant we should try to design a project that could be built for around that much, which we did.

That relates to what I call project risk - basically the risks posed to a project if it is too complex or expensive for a city to be able to digest. We designed the BIG U to be digestible for HUD and New York City - and that's why we were able to do so well in the competition.

+ The concept of project risk is a part of the *Designing with Risk* course you teach at the University of Pennsylvania [Penn]. What exactly does project risk mean and how should it shape the design process?

Project risk is basically just a way to describe all things that can undermine a project–from conceptual design to construction. It includes financial risk, contract risk, political risk, legal risk, reputational risk, engineering risk, design risk–all these things are embedded in a project. The reason I find it so important is that if you want to get projects done, if you want to build things, then you have to think about how all the different actors in the life of a project approach these risks to shape its outcome. Oftentimes, the way that financial or contract or political risk is managed on a project plays a much bigger role in its outcome than more global or existential risks like climate change that the project seeks to address.

As we move into an era of incredible uncertainty, as a result of climate change and global political instability, the challenge for designers will be in thinking through the

East Side Coastal Resilience project, concept design. View of Delancey Street Bridge: current situation, proposed, proposed during storm surge.

ways in which we can scope projects that are manageable and that respond to both those types of risk: global risks and project risks. That's the only way to design a project that, once built, can live up to the promises made in your renderings and become a building block for long-term adaptation. There's no real culture of integrated planning in this country – resiliency and adaptation are not built through big plans that are pursued methodically over time. It's all built through individual projects. So, understanding the risks inherent to our projects, as part of a long-term vision, is crucial to building resilience in the United States.

+ That's a good segue into the rest of your work outside of the RBD competition, both here at Penn and in partnership with the Rockefeller Foundation, because so much of it is based on transitioning from the design culture of Holland to that of the US. What's been most jarring about your move across the Atlantic?

I've been working in the United States for three years now and there's a number of things that have been pretty striking. The first takeaway is that when I came here as a Dutch person I thought that after Storm Sandy, people would get serious about protecting all their stuff. They didn't. But then I was introduced to this notion of resilience, which is fantastic and, in many ways, uniquely American. When understood correctly, resilience is premised on the idea that our urban environments are complex adaptive systems that we simply cannot control. Flood protection in Holland is about degrees of control – so the unwillingness or inability of the US to try and control its risk like we have, even after Sandy, was a surprise. We have a thousand years of controlling nature in the Netherlands [even though we are now 'building with' it] – nothing like that exists here [in the US]. Once you recognize that you have to design within and for complex adaptive systems, it means that you have to take a systems approach to coastal design. That's why I'm very happy to have landed in landscape architecture at Penn, because the whole department is organized around understanding how to strategically intervene in complex systems like cities.

One thing that's different for me—maybe because I'm a pragmatic Dutch and also an architect by training—is that I tend to view systems less as moral constructs than landscape architects often do. I tend to view things like social principles, material flows, and financial mechanisms as more descriptive, whereas the designers I work with here have a much stronger philosophical position on those things – what constitutes the right amount of balance or whatever in the system. But where my class at Penn intersects with that is that I ask students to think about risk in as broad a sense as possible. We move from sociologists like Ulrich Beck and Eric Klinenberg to very technical readings on structural engineering and actuarial science, and then around to Donella Meadows and other systems theorists – all before we ask them to design anything.

Another takeaway is that, in a country that doesn't have any [integrated] planning or vision, it's crucial for designers to understand debt. Especially on the East Coast, understanding the way that debt dictates the future – by that I mean the ability to finance and insure and otherwise capitalize projects is the key to identifying the role that design can play in analyzing, communicating, and dealing with risk. It's what shapes the potential futures for cities along the coast and, as a result, it's what determines which projects get built and which ones get discarded.

Lastly, I think the other takeaway is that designing with risk will increasingly mean that we must design things that are not necessarily physical objects. They might be digital platforms, they might be new development policies, they might be social cohesion-building programs. That's where we spend most of our time in my course, trying to think through what it means to design processes and policies instead of objects – and you can't do that without designing at the system scale.

+ Most professional design associations [like the AIA and ASLA] fetishize object-driven design at the expense of what you're describing. So how do you work through the tension between how the mainstream of architecture and landscape architecture view design and the way you're approaching it through Penn and your work at One?

Well the thing about my course at Penn is that it's taken by landscape architects, architects, and city planners, so it's not really wed to any of those design ideologies – it's interdisciplinary. I don't feel beholden to anyone else's view of what design is or isn't in there. At One, we've organized the practice to try and respond to the project risks that I mentioned earlier. We don't have much sole-authorship, nor do I think we have any real signature to our work even though many of the projects we take on are internationally recognized. I don't want, or believe in harnessing, the degree of control it takes to maintain a brand like that. It can be a powerful thing, but I don't want any part of that approach to design.

I don't really believe in the idea of positioning yourself as a signature architect – it's too much work and, for the kinds of problems I'm interested in solving, it isn't very effective. To do the kind of work I'm interested in, it's better to lose your signature or that instant recognition of authorship because resilience is too complex a concept to be both attainable and to permit that sort of design. I realized when I became well known as an architect [with the design of a daycare center] at 25 or 26, which is ridiculously young, that if I didn't make a concerted effort to break with that tradition of establishing a signature and building a brand around it that I would be designing daycare centers for the rest of my life. That kind of design has never interested me.

+ What else has shaped the trajectory of your approach to designing with risk?

Well I think, at the very least, they're all connected to this concept of resilience – which can be considered uniquely American as a cultural construct. I understand the need to work through projects here, but I also understand that, at the end of the day, design practice has to be about more than the simple assemblage of projects into a portfolio. It has to be about those projects adding up to something greater than their individual parts – to something that can change the world.

That's how we have organized One, in which we also do unsolicited projects to fill these gaps, and why I've been working to develop a resilience certificate here at Penn, work with Rockefeller's 100 Resilient Cities on the [Chief Resilience Officer] curriculum, and with RBD and a number of design schools on a network we call RBD-U. Resilience, as a metaphor, should be forcing all of us to rethink the nature of design education and Penn is very quickly becoming the center of that restructuring.

I think that developing a new educational model–and organizing a community of designers at Penn and beyond–is very exciting, and the exact right response to everything that RBD and NDRC has taught me. It's the best platform that I can envision for translating all of the lessons from those initiatives–along with things like Rockefeller's 100 Resilient Cities program–into new design knowledge that we can export out of those communities and across the globe through better design.

+ What else should the readers of LA+ know about the ways in which risk and resilience can, or should, reshape design culture?

The most important thing to me is to remember that resilience is more than just a metaphor for designing projects – it's a way for me to structure my approach to practice and research more broadly. The same principles that we tried to integrate into the BIG U are the same ones I use to go after and manage projects at One. Resilience can make our individual projects better, sure, but it can also make our firms and our design culture better if we embed those principles more firmly into practice.

That's why this RBD-U network is so important – it breaks away from the narrow definition of resilience as a thing to do in coastal cities or in response to climate change. It is so much more than that. But at its most fundamental level, it's about creating networks and redundancy – and we hope to use the concept as a way to rethink what it means to be a design school in the 21st century.

VISUAL ESSAYS

Deepwater Horizon Oil Spill, May 24, 2010

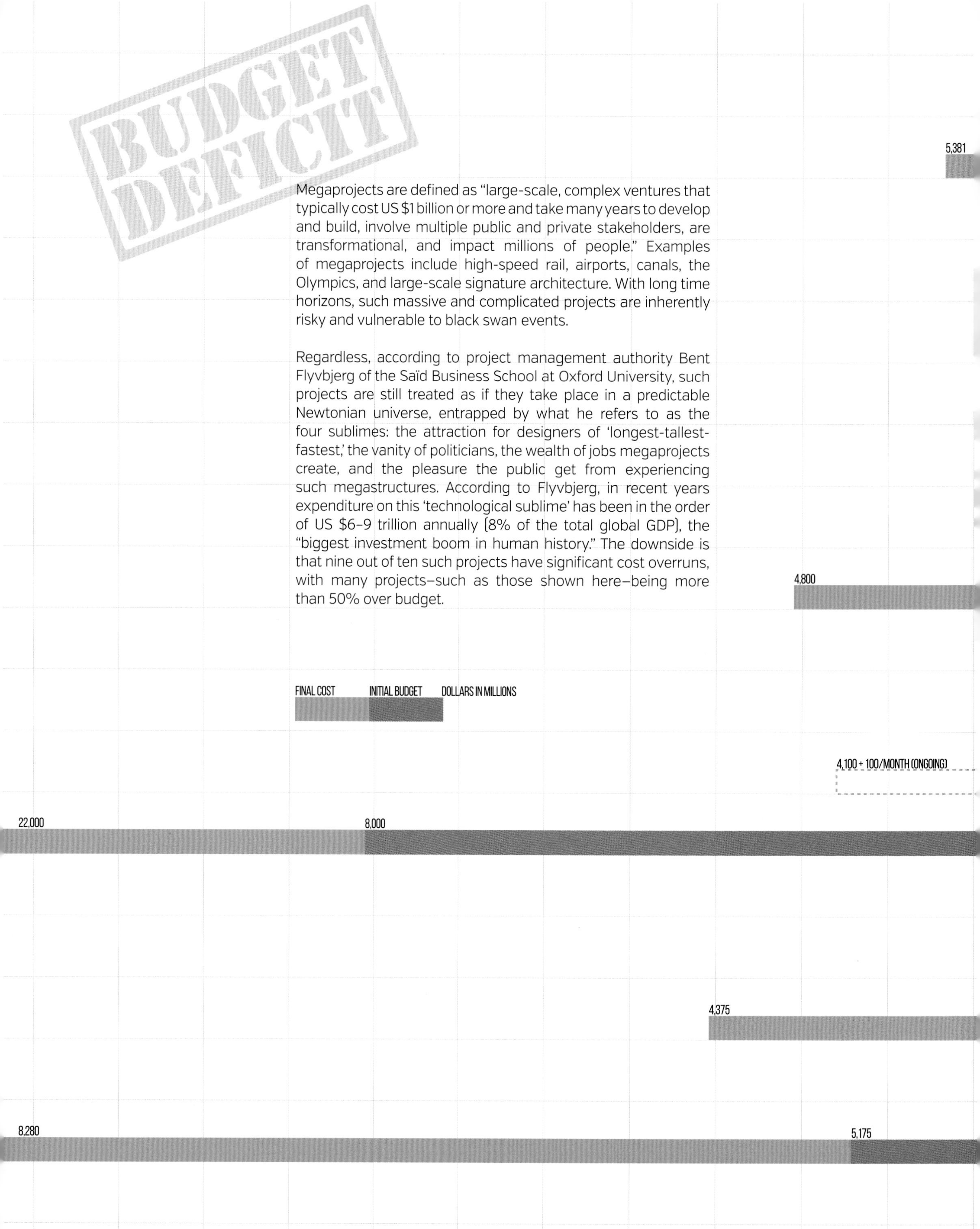

Megaprojects are defined as "large-scale, complex ventures that typically cost US $1 billion or more and take many years to develop and build, involve multiple public and private stakeholders, are transformational, and impact millions of people." Examples of megaprojects include high-speed rail, airports, canals, the Olympics, and large-scale signature architecture. With long time horizons, such massive and complicated projects are inherently risky and vulnerable to black swan events.

Regardless, according to project management authority Bent Flyvbjerg of the Saïd Business School at Oxford University, such projects are still treated as if they take place in a predictable Newtonian universe, entrapped by what he refers to as the four sublimes: the attraction for designers of 'longest-tallest-fastest,' the vanity of politicians, the wealth of jobs megaprojects create, and the pleasure the public get from experiencing such megastructures. According to Flyvbjerg, in recent years expenditure on this 'technological sublime' has been in the order of US $6–9 trillion annually (8% of the total global GDP), the "biggest investment boom in human history." The downside is that nine out of ten such projects have significant cost overruns, with many projects—such as those shown here—being more than 50% over budget.

Source: Bent Flyvbjerg, "What You Should Know about Megaprojects and Why: An Overview," *Project Management Journal* 2 (2014): 6–14.

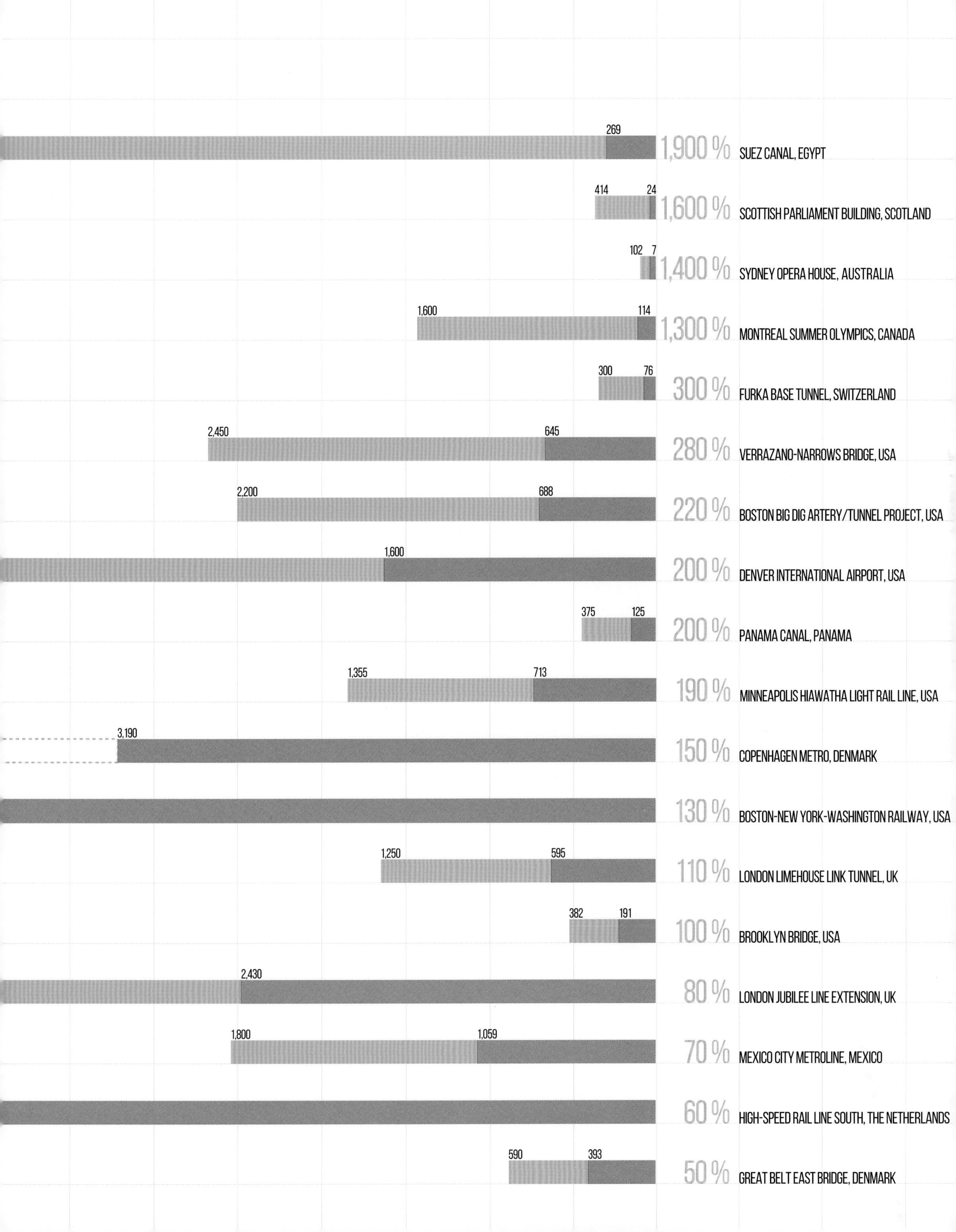

269
1,900 %
SUEZ CANAL, EGYPT
414
24
1,600 %
SCOTTISH PARLIAMENT BUILDING, SCOTLAND
102
7
1,400 %
SYDNEY OPERA HOUSE, AUSTRALIA
1,600
114
1,300 %
MONTREAL SUMMER OLYMPICS, CANADA
300
76
300 %
FURKA BASE TUNNEL, SWITZERLAND
2,450
645
280 %
VERRAZANO-NARROWS BRIDGE, USA
2,200
688
220 %
BOSTON BIG DIG ARTERY/TUNNEL PROJECT, USA
1,600
200 %
DENVER INTERNATIONAL AIRPORT, USA
375
125
200 %
PANAMA CANAL, PANAMA
1,355
713
190 %
MINNEAPOLIS HIAWATHA LIGHT RAIL LINE, USA
3,190
150 %
COPENHAGEN METRO, DENMARK
130 %
BOSTON-NEW YORK-WASHINGTON RAILWAY, USA
1,250
595
110 %
LONDON LIMEHOUSE LINK TUNNEL, UK
382
191
100 %
BROOKLYN BRIDGE, USA
2,430
80 %
LONDON JUBILEE LINE EXTENSION, UK
1,800
1,059
70 %
MEXICO CITY METROLINE, MEXICO
60 %
HIGH-SPEED RAIL LINE SOUTH, THE NETHERLANDS
590
393
50 %
GREAT BELT EAST BRIDGE, DENMARK

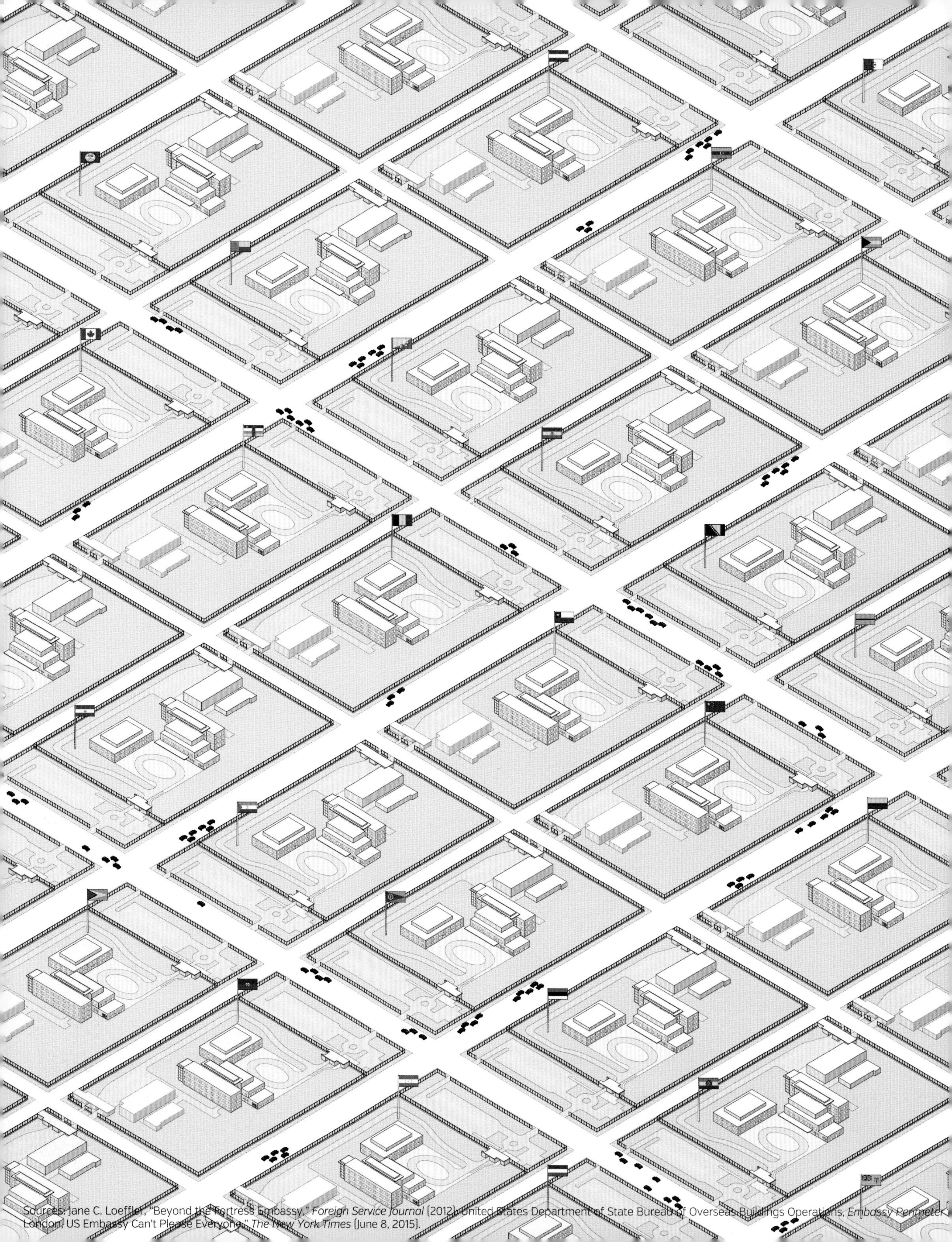

Sources: Jane C. Loeffler, "Beyond the Fortress Embassy," *Foreign Service Journal* (2012); United States Department of State Bureau of Overseas Buildings Operations, *Embassy Perimeter*
London, US Embassy Can't Please Everyone," *The New York Times* (June 8, 2015).

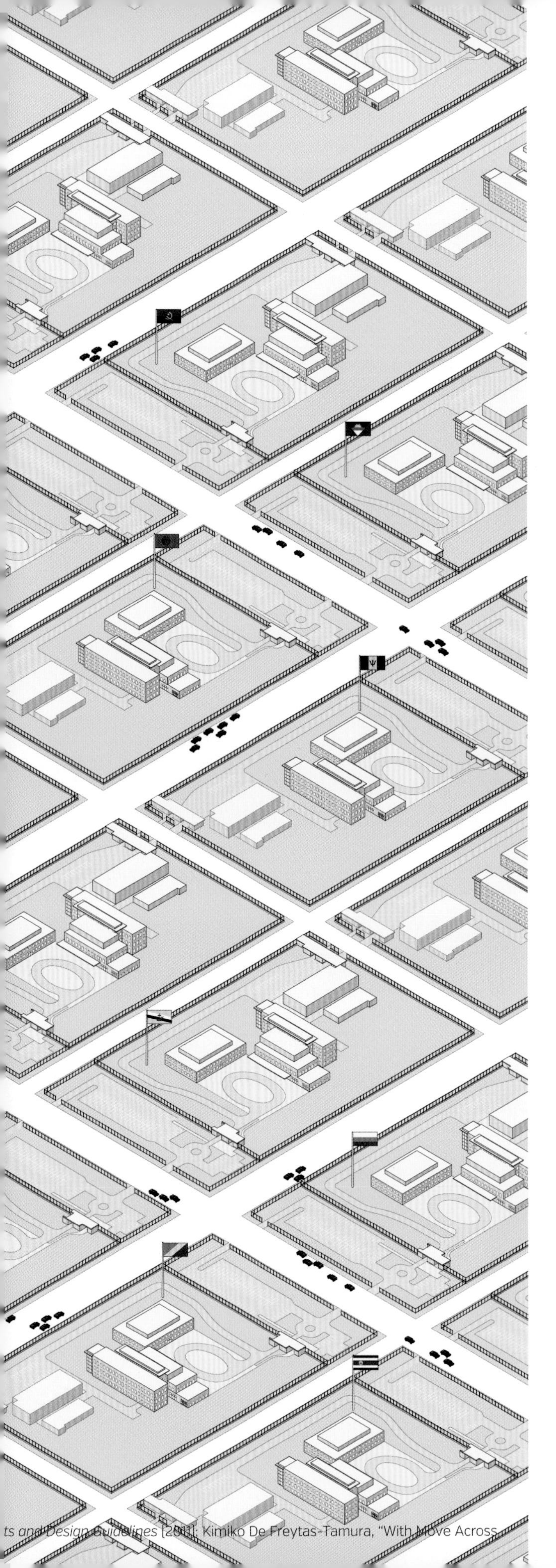

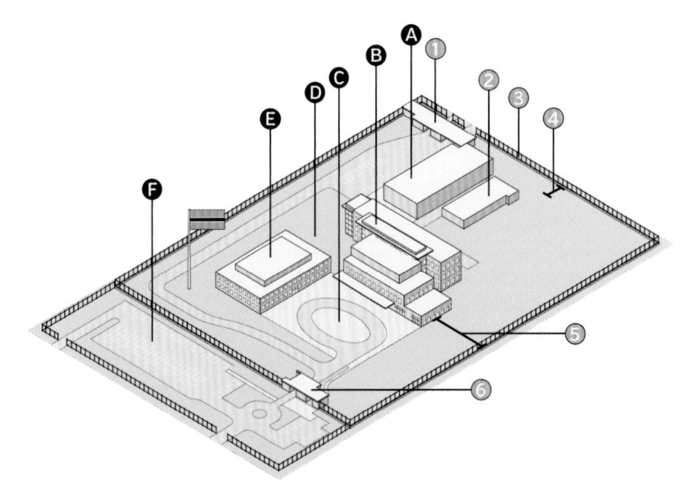

MAJOR EMBASSY SECURITY FEATURES

1. Service entry access control
2. Security guards' living quarters
3. 9' minimum height anti-ram and anti-climb perimeter fencing
4. 20' clear zone at perimeter fence
5. 100' minimum setbacks from perimeter fencing
6. Main entry access control

OTHER MAJOR EMBASSY ELEMENTS

- A General services office
- B Main embassy building
- C Entry courtyard
- D Embassy garden
- E Embassy annex
- F Employee and visitor parking

DIPLOTOPIA

Increasing security standards for embassy design in response to the proliferation of targeted attacks against US diplomatic outposts have resulted in the embrace of fortress-like facilities that are symbolically, programmatically, and physically detached from the urban contexts of their host nations. Recent efforts to minimize the visual impact of security measures and help embassies better integrate with local communities–such as at the new US Embassy in London–have met with mixed reactions from locals and design critics.

Rather than trying to strike a compromise between security, design quality, and cultural connection, Diplotopia proposes a new future for diplomacy, creating a consolidated location in which diplomats from all 193 UN member nations may safely conduct their diplomatic missions. Each nation would be given its own embassy based upon the US Standard Embassy Design [pictured above], allowing for rapid and efficient construction of the city while adhering to the most stringent standards for security and safety.

Sources: "The Internet's Undersea World," *The Guardian* (October 13, 2011); NOAA Office of Coast Survey, "Navigational Boating Chart 12324," http://www.charts.noaa.gov/OnLineViewer/12324.shtml; Michael Sechrist, *Cyberspace in Deep Water: Protecting Undersea Communication Cables* (Harvard Kennedy School of Government, 2010); TeleGeography, "Interactive Submarine Cable Map," https://www.telegeography.com/telecom-maps/submarine-cable-map.1.html; April Glaser, "The feds' plan to protect the Internet's oceanic backbone from typhoons and cyberattacks," *Fusion*, July 13, 2016.

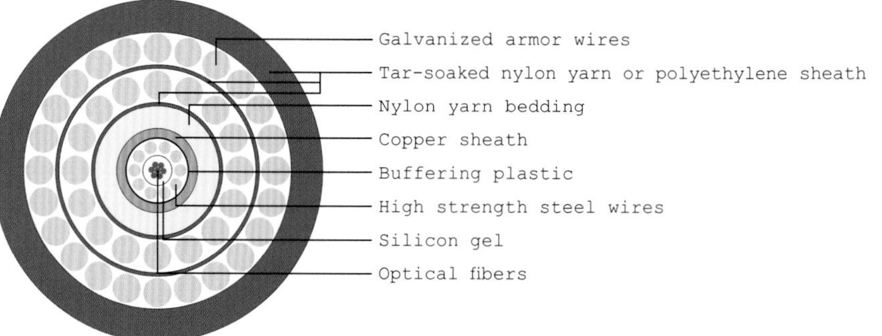

TYPICAL UNDERSEA CABLE SECTION
SCALE: 1:1

LANDFALL

MANASQUAN, NEW JERSEY

Within the frame of this image, the Apollo, TAT 14, and Gemini Bermuda undersea fiber optic cables make landfall. Ninety-five percent of global telephone and internet activity relies upon a network of 293 undersea cables like these. The cable network is responsible for $10 trillion of financial transactions every day and the world's militaries rely on it for everything from daily communication to transmitting unmanned aerial vehicle video. Yet the physical cables remain largely unprotected, susceptible to damage from boats, extreme weather events, and seismic activity, as well as intentional interference.

Due to oceanic conditions, commercial boat routes and critical service areas, the landing points of cables tend to tightly cluster in close proximity to one another. The location above is one of nine landing points clustered near New York City. Such areas of tight geographic clustering represent points of greatest physical vulnerability within this critical global network.

THE THIRD POLE

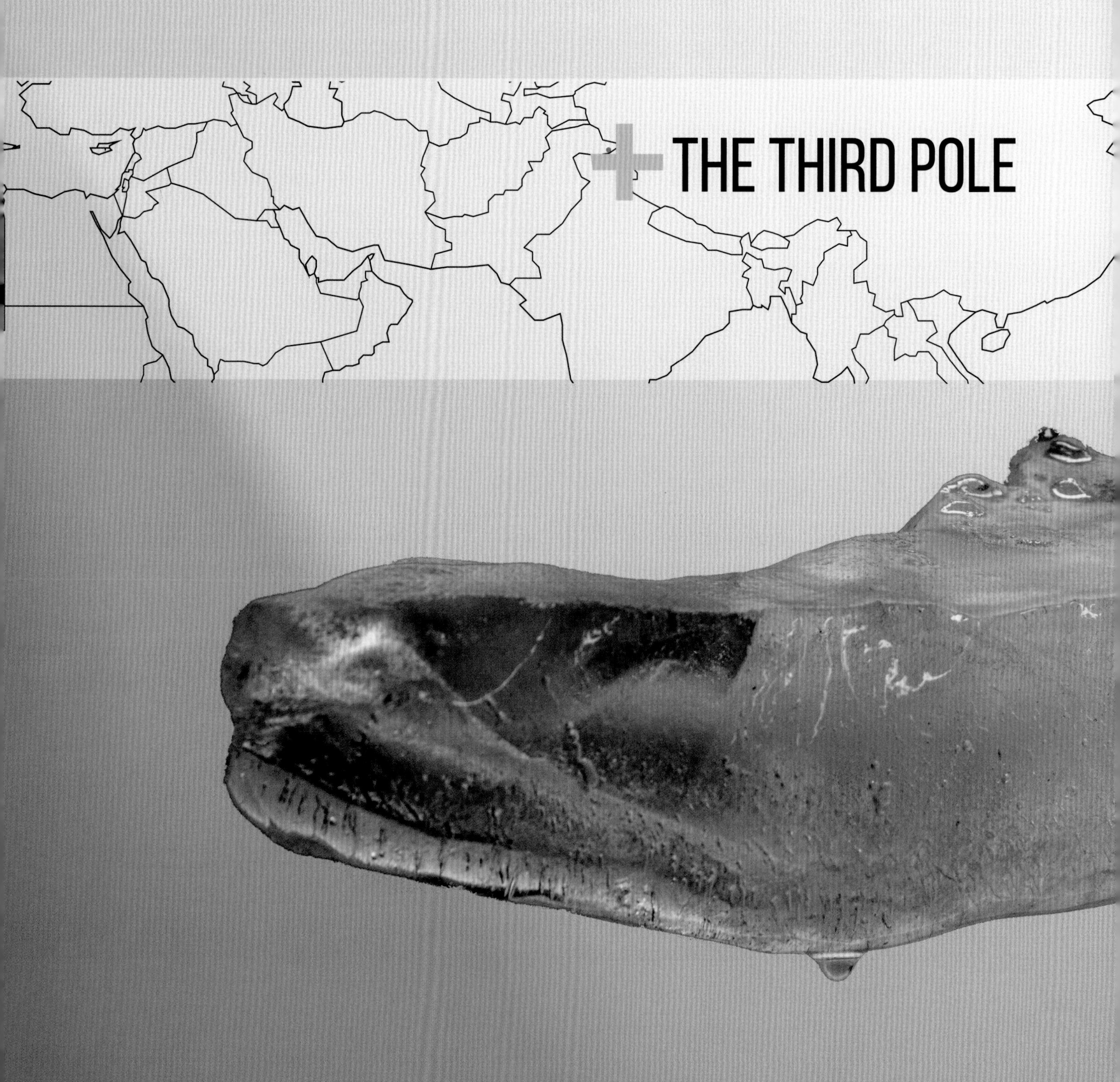

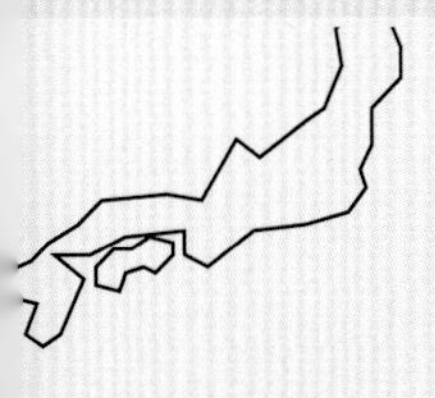

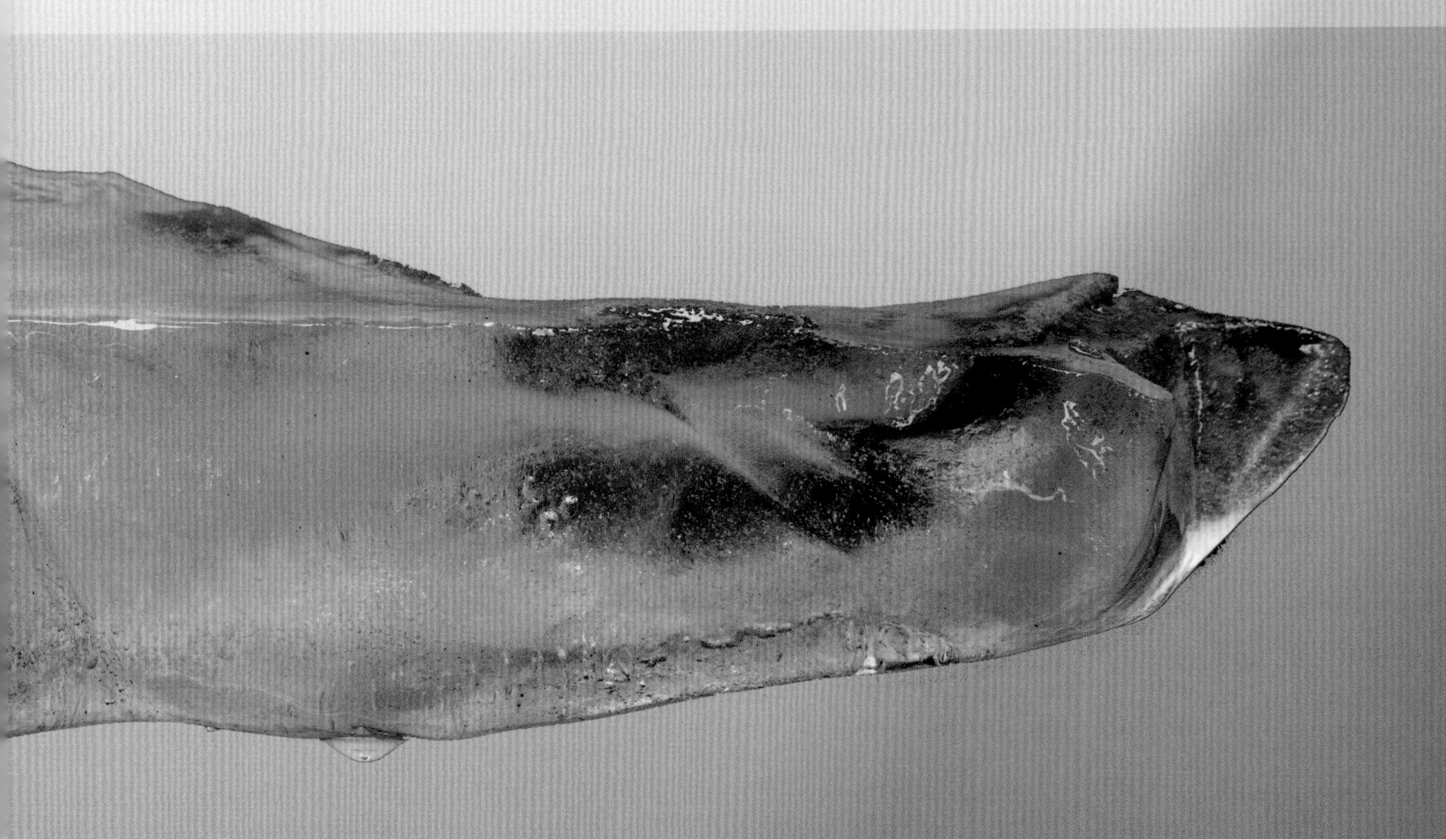

The Siachen Glacier is the largest glacier outside of the North and South Pole. With an area of almost 1000 km2, it sits within a larger ice field that encompasses the Tibetan Plateau and Himalayan-Hindu Kush mountain range, collectively known as the Third Pole. Melt from the Siachen Glacier flows into the Ganga, Indus, and Brahmaputra floodplains, the world's largest irrigation network, supporting over a billion people and making it one of most important natural resource assets in Asia. Claims to the glacier's sovereignty has made it a site of military conflict between India and Pakistan since 1984, with over 2000 amassed deaths as a result of armed combat and the harsh terrain.

In 2007, officials at the United Nation's Intergovernmental Panel on Climate Change boldly claimed that due to global warming the Third Pole could disappear by 2035 if not earlier. Although this timeline has since been extended, the glacier is melting. Each droplet gives life to the delta below, but also, inexorably, takes it away.

[Image] Ice cast in a 22"x10" mold of a digitally modeled replica of the Saichen Glacier.

Sources: B. Rabus & O. Lang, "Ice Motion and Topography in the Siachen Glacier Area, Central Kashmir, Derived with an Operational Processing System for INSAR-DEMs," German Aerospace Center DLR, January 2000, 2. https://www.researchgate.net/publication/255615309; Ab. Sethi., and T. Jalan, "Two Soldiers Die Every Month in Saichen," The Wire (December 2016); P. Bagla, "IPCC Finally Acknowledges its Himalayan Blunder," https://blogs.scientificamerican.com/guest-blog/ipcc-finally-acknowledges-its-e2809chimalayan-blundere2809d/

2017
2018
2021
2022
2025
2026
2029
2030
2033
2034

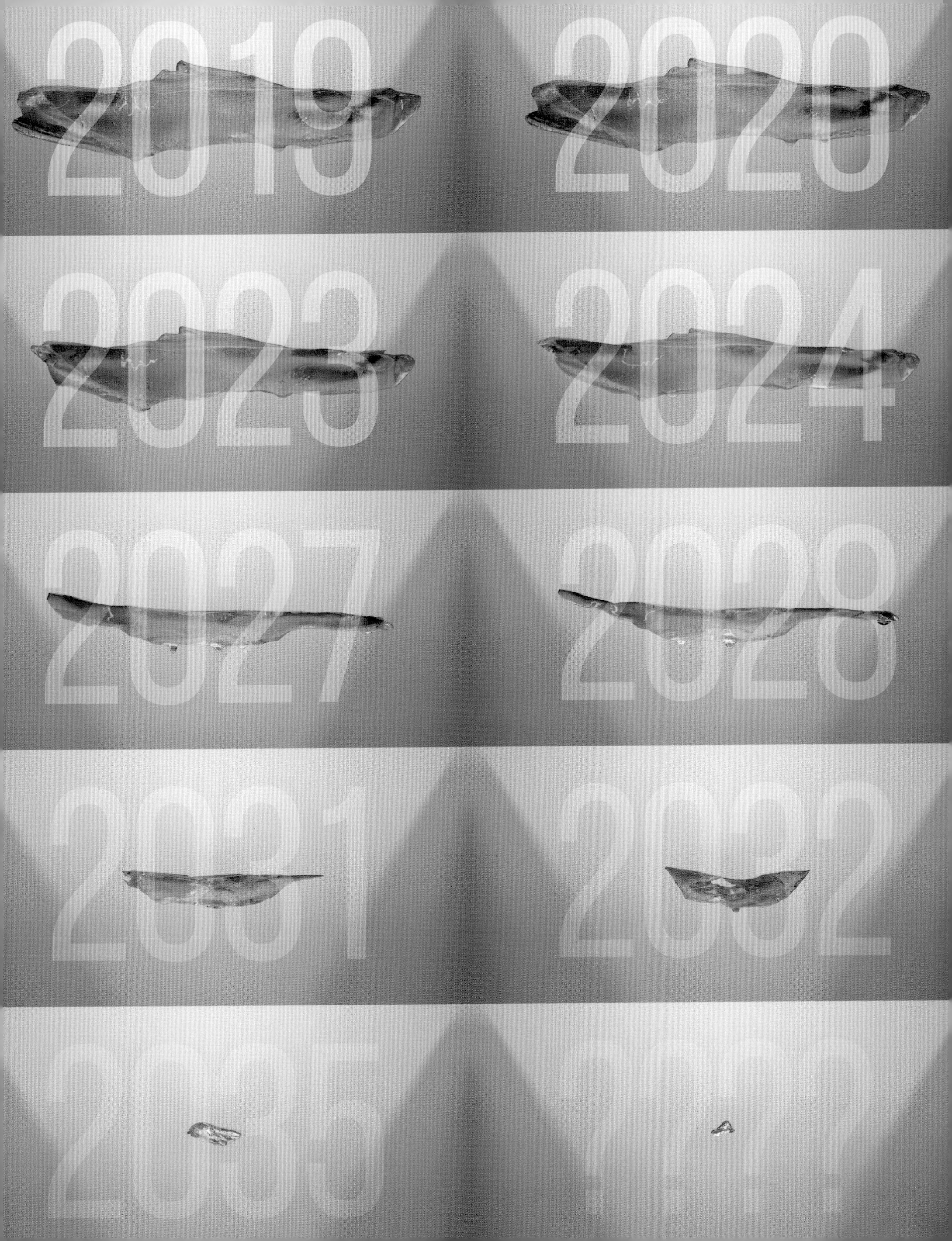
2019
2020
2023
2024
2027
2028
2031
2032
2035

GROUNDSCRAPER

LOCATION: UNKNOWN

In times of trouble the troubled dig in. Originally built by Phrygians and later inhabited by Christians escaping persecution, there are over 200 labyrinthine underground cities in the Derinkuyu district in Nevşehir Province, Turkey. The modern incarnations of this troglodytic urbanism are the undisclosed bombproof bunker complexes designed to accommodate the political and military elite in most of the world's political capitals. Probably the largest example is Dixia Cheng underneath Beijing. With over 85 square kilometers of living spaces, Dixia Cheng was designed to accommodate 300,000 people. Portions of Dixia Cheng are today occupied by nearly one million migrant workers, known locally as the Rat Tribe.

Underground urbanism is now increasingly available on the free market. Luxurious multi-million-dollar underground 'survival' condos are being designed in undisclosed locations in South Dakota, Kansas, Germany, and the Czech Republic. And these are no mere concrete bunkers; as well as spacious apartments, many developments boast swimming pools, theaters, exercise rooms, restaurants, bakeries, wine cellars, classrooms, and hospital facilities. For those with the means to buy into these below-ground survivalist communities, the risk of the coming apocalypse–at least in the mind of the consumer–is greatly reduced. A new Rat Tribe is digging in.

Sources: Sang Ye & Geremie Barmé, "Beijing Underground: An Invisible City," China Heritage Quarterly [2008]: 14; Jim Dobson, "Inside the world's largest private apocalypse shelter, The Oppidum," Forbes [November 5, 2015]; Sophie Jane Evans, "The ultimate doomsday escape," DailyMail.com [June 15, 2015].

IMAGE CREDITS

Endpapers

"The Tower of Babel" by Pieter Bruegal (c. 1563) via Wikimedia Commons, public domain.

Editorial

p. 4: "Vince's Head" by the National Museum of American History, used under CC-BY-NC-SA 2.0 license via flickr.com.

The Politics of Risk

p. 6: "Trump Roulette" by, and courtesy of, Clay Gruber.

p. 11: "Life Lotto" by, and courtesy of, Clay Gruber.

Toward a Transparent Planet

p. 12–13: "Luuq, Somalia" © Planet Inc., courtesy Andrew Zolli.

p. 14: "Container Ship Jessica B" by Raimond Spekking used under CC BY-SA 4.0 license via Wikimedia Commons (altered).

p. 15: Image by, and courtesy of Clay Gruber.

Acts of Gods

p. 16: "Airplane window night view" by Andreas Ubbe Dall, used with permission (altered).

p. 18: "Earth System" by, and courtesy of, Wesley Chiang.

p. 21-25: Images by, and courtesy of, Chieh Huang, Wesley Chiang, and Richard Weller.

Risk, Uncertainty, and the Inevitability of Rapid Sea Level Rise

p. 26–27: "Rain at Ocean Beach" by Brocken Inaglory, used under CC BY-SA license via Wikimedia Commons.

p. 29–30: Images by, and courtesy of, Kristina Hill.

Retrench/Rise Up

p. 32: "Subgrade Flushing Tunnel Model at Norton Basin, Rockaway Peninsula, New York" by, and courtesy of, Catherine Seavitt Nordenson/Structures of Coastal Resilience (flow lines added).

p. 35: "Satellite View of Venice" by NASA, public domain (flow lines added).

p. 37: "Little Egg Marsh Island and The Raunt, Jamaica Bay" by Vertical Aerial Photography for Structures of Coastal Resilience, courtesy of Catherine Seavitt Nordenson (flow lines added).

America's Petrochemical Garden

p. 38–39: "Damage from Hurricane Ike in Bolivar Peninsula, Texas" by Jocelyn Augustino/FEMA, public domain (altered).

p. 40: Mapping by Nick McClintock and Billy Fleming, courtesy of Billy Fleming.

p. 42–43: Historical images of Galveston, Texas, courtesy of the Galveston and Texas History Center in the Rosenberg Library.

p. 45: Infographic by Nick McClintock, Billy Fleming, and Sean McKay, courtesy of Billy Fleming.

In Conversation with Stephen Kieran + James Timberlake

p. 48: Portraits of Stephen Kieran and James Timberlake by Ed Wheeler, courtesy of KieranTimberlake.

p. 50–57: Images from *Alluvium: Dhaka, Bangladesh in the Crossroads of Water*, courtesy of KieranTimberlake.

Living with Risk

p. 58: "Tsunami Protection Wall at Hamaoka Nuclear Power Station" by Chubu Electric Power Company from the Japan Society of Civil Engineers 2015 Awards.

p. 60–61: Image © Kate Crawford, Resilient Urbanism.

Resilient Urbanism 2.0

p. 62: Image by, and courtesy of, Wesley Chiang.

p. 65: Rendering of Masterplan for Hans Tavsens Park and Koorsgard, Norrebro, Copenhagen © SLA/Beauty and the Bit.

p. 66: Rendering of proposed US Embassy in London by, and courtesy of, KieranTimberlake.

Extreme Landscapes: A 21st-Century Sublime

p. 68: Image by Elvis Wong.

p. 71: "Damage to Christchurch Cathedral following the 2011 Earthquakes" by, and courtesy of, Jacky Bowring.

No Risk, No Play

p. 72: "The Sad Effects of Climbing Trees" from *The Accidents of Youth* (1819), public domain.

Managing Risk in the Energyshed

p. 74–75: "America's Watershed" by, and courtesy of, Clay Gruber.

p. 78: "Mapping of the PJM Backbone Transmission System" by, and courtesy of, Clay Gruber.

Fluxes of Risk

p. 81: "Smog puts Dozens of Chinese Cities of Red Alert" (December 2016) by Joshua Stevens/NASA, public domain (altered).

p. 83: "Vertical Farm Installation at the Palais De Tokyo, Paris 2015" by diephotodesigner.de, courtesy of INFARM.

p. 84–85: Images of Particle Wave Project by, and courtesy of, Elaine Laguerta, Grant Saita, Joe Burg, and Kyle O'Konis.

Designed for Disease?

p. 86: Image by, and courtesy of, Clay Gruber.

p. 88: "Zika Virus Capsid" by Thomas Splettstoesser, via Wikimedia Commons under CC-BY license.

p. 91: Image by, and courtesy of, Clay Gruber using mosquito image via Wikimedia Commons, public domain.

What Doesn't Kill You

p. 92: Screen capture from *The Trial* (1962), directed by Orson Welles, public domain.

p. 95: "Fortune and Her Wheel" from Boccaccio's *De Casibus Virorum Illustrium* (1467), public domain (image altered).

In Conversation with Matthijs Bouw

p. 96: Portrait by Eljee Bergwerff, courtesy of Matthijs Bouw (image altered).

p. 99: Images of East Side Coastal Resilience project, concept design by BIG/One Architecture, courtesy of Matthijs Bouw.

Visual Essays

p. 103: "Deepwater Horizon Oil Spill - May 24, 2010" by NASA/Goddard Space Flight Center, public domain (altered).

Budget Deficit

p. 104–105: Image by, and courtesy of, Wesley Chiang, using data from Bent Flyvbjerg's *What You Should Know about Megaprojects and Why* (2014).

Diplotopia

p. 106-107: Image by, and courtesy of, Sean McKay.

Landfall

p. 98: Image by, and courtesy of, Sean McKay.

Third Pole

p. 110-113: Images and base model by, and courtesy of, Clay Gruber incorporating photographs by Casey Egner and Clay Gruber.

Groundscraper

p. 114-115: Image by, and courtesy of, Elvis Wong.

IN THE NEXT ISSUE OF

LA+

Paradisiacal, utopian, dystopian, heterotopian – islands hold an especially enigmatic and beguiling place in our imagination. Issue 07 of LA+ Journal brings you the results of the **LA+ IMAGINATION** open international design ideas competition, in which we asked designers to create a new island. In addition to showcasing the winners and other interesting, unusual, or surprising entries, **LA+ IMAGINATION** features interviews with jurors James Corner, Richard Weller, Marion Weiss, Javier Arpa, Matthew Gandy, and Mark Kingwell.

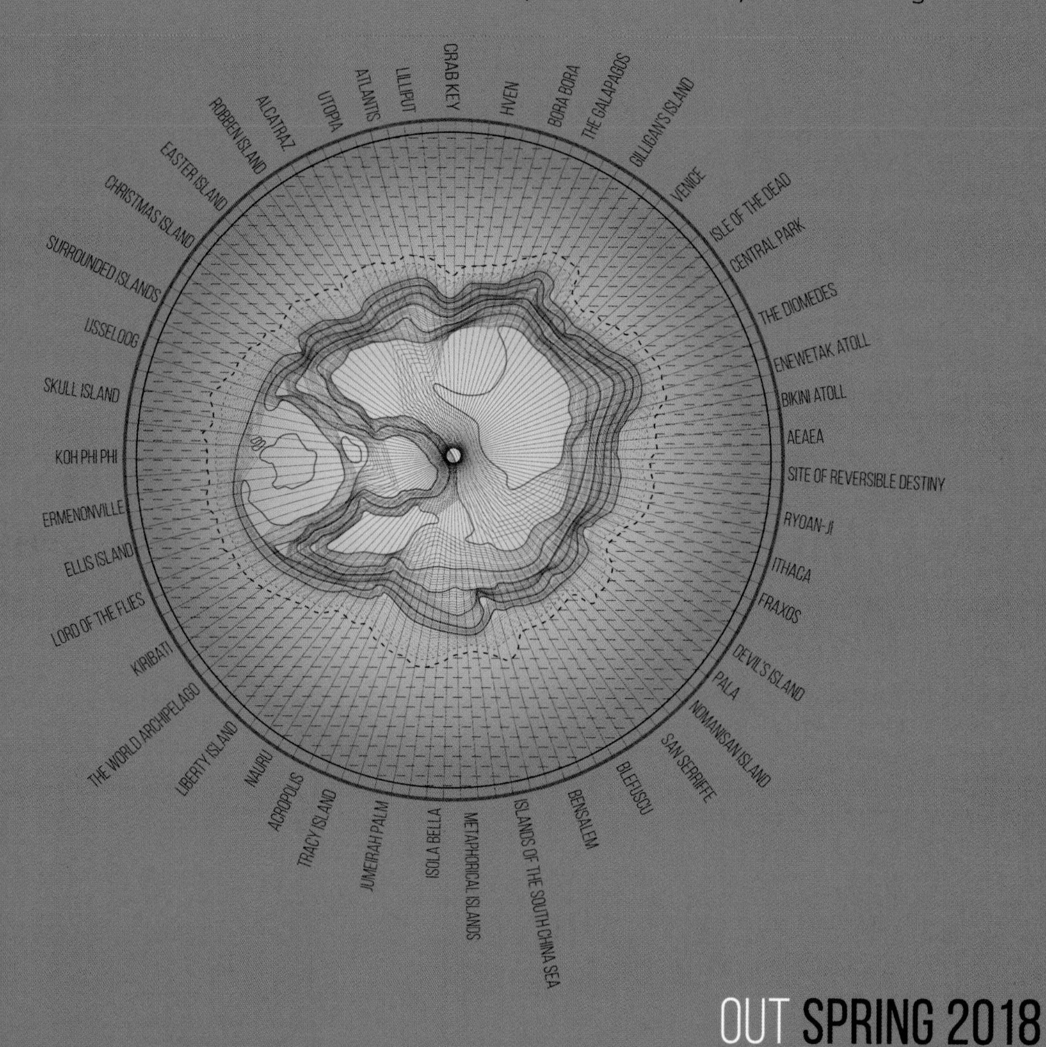

OUT **SPRING 2018**

LA+
WILD SPRING 2015

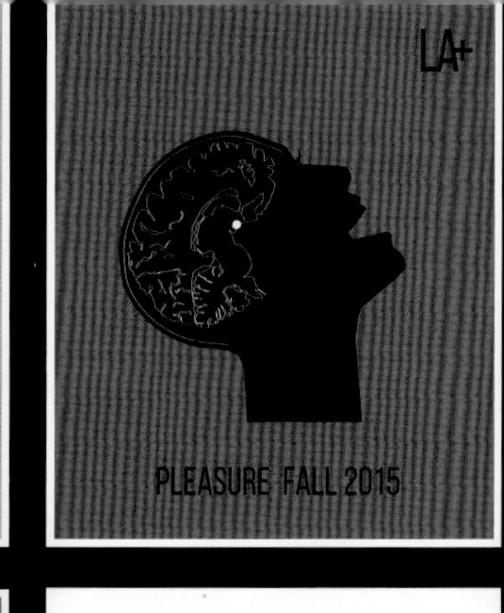
LA+
PLEASURE FALL 2015

LA+
TYRANNY SPRING 2016

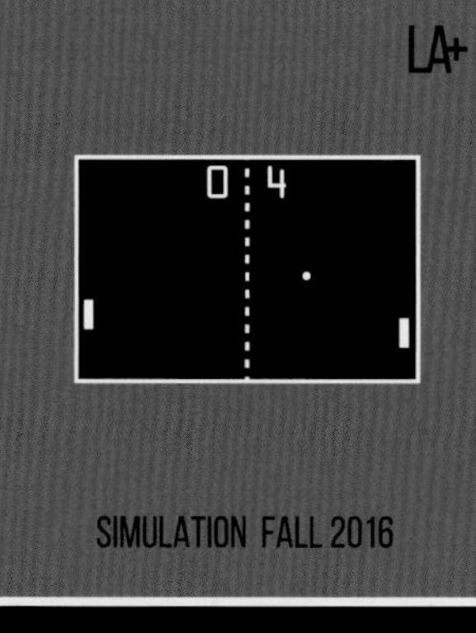
LA+
0 4
SIMULATION FALL 2016

LA+
INTERDISCIPLINARY JOURNAL
OF LANDSCAPE ARCHITECTURE

LA+
IDENTITY SPRING 2017

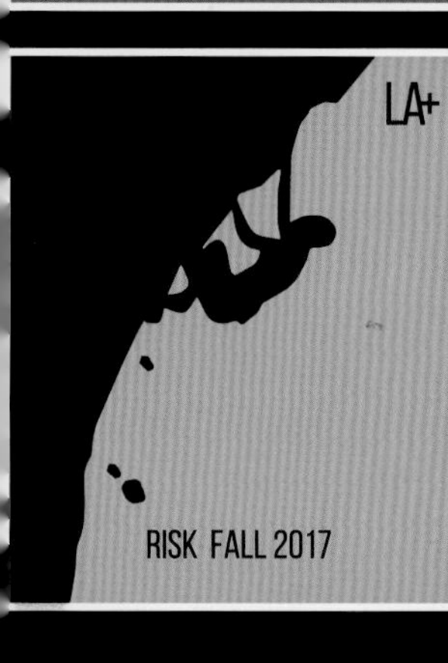
LA+
RISK FALL 2017

LA+
IMAGINATION SPRING 2018

LA+
TIME FALL 2018